Feelings Of The Heart

Part 2

Darlene G Williams

PublishAmerica
Baltimore

First printing

ISBN: 1-4137-4391-9
PUBLISHED BY PUBLISHAMERICA, LLLP
www.publishamerica.com
Baltimore

Printed in the United States of America

Preface

Feelings of the Heart: Part Two is the second addition. It seals tightly those emotions that are trapped within. This book sends signals to the mind again and again. Challenging thoughts, which are bone chilling as well as revealing, at the same time reaching out to comfort in areas that needs healing. A book of poetry that goes to another level beyond the simple term of understanding. It leaves your heart rushing and dancing. It's about real life tragedies, suffering, and making a change to ease your pain. Yet it's about love and kindness that's gentle to the soul, but not letting go of the almighty that truly holds. The fact our destiny is beyond our control. Reality helps teach lessons in a world that's motionless and cold. *Feelings of the Heart: Part Two* without a doubt will touch you and console.

A PHASE

To look in a mirror closely at one's self
To take a pinch of feeling,
To really care for someone else.
Time shatters upon your head
Bleeding your soul,
On who should brake bread.
Is it really peaceful sleep in another's bed.
Only in honesty will your needs be fed
The strong is really the weakest,
When trying to survive.
Especially when you're hit,
With the truth from your blind side!

Contents

Feelings Of The Heart

Part 2

ABOUT THANKSGIVING

Let me share with you about Thanksgiving Day
It is celebrated in so many ways;
The gift of love stays the same.
A lot of people look at Thanksgiving
As a day the Indians
Broke bread with the pilgrims;
However, this part of it is true.
Our history has so much it has been through
Just like everyday not only on Thanksgiving
It should be remembered because Jesus
Has risen
We tend to forget exactly what was given
Even the fact we're among the living
Remember how important it is to give
Always care what others feel
The hunger of a mammal's soul would kill
Everyone is not fortunate to get a good meal
So tear the word Thanksgiving in two parts;
One for the ending and one to start.
In plain English it's saying, open your heart
Thanks means to be grateful,
Giving means share from the heart delightful
To think about only one's self is spiteful!

AFFLICTION

Nailing my skin over and over to floor
My body covered in blistered sores
Red ants bite me again and again
Maggots imbedded in my skin
Crows swoop down to steal my flesh
Life won't leave this invested nest
Misery and darkness gives me a kiss
Suffering and burden says I won't be missed
Misfortune clouds have always hovered over me
Never ever letting me be
Blinded by the truth and refused to see
Reality will never pack up and leave
Smothered by my will,
Mr. Breath feels, I have no right to live
Lying there playing a film of my life
I wish I had took time to think twice
Cooking that spoon frosty black
Melting down that rock call crack
My mind has truly went out of whack
The light burns my eyes like a bat
Running from the law
Like a rat runs from a cat
Selling my child, so I can get high
I can hear her screams and cries
Saying, mommy, mommy, just tell me why?
I hate I had to tell her lies
He's ripped her vagina wide open,
There hanging is her clitoris
My baby's body is now part of his required list
In order for me to get that hit
All his needs must be met
He don't want me anymore,
Not even to suck his dick

My body trembling and shaking for that fix
Every time puts me at a greater risk
That blow isn't pure
It's always mixed
I'm dirty and poor
While making him rich
Now I'm dying because I'm sick
Countless times, I've been in jail
Now earth gives away to the flames of hell
Mr. Life finally puts up bail
Saying goodbye to this wasted shell
Nothings left now, but the rusty nails!

AN IMMORAL ACT

To steal something precious inside
To take their joy and pride,
The hidden secret of their other side.
It's hard to reach out
You just want to blame
People don't understand
Open your heart to share their pain.
Reach out and touch the burning flames
But first you must walk through their shame
Pretend it's your mother or daughter
Victims their name...
Early departed virtue
I have to show the men through.
Men see from a different angle
The word rape,
The male chauvinist can't truly relate.
What if you were to be castrated?
No longer able to masturbate
Now, nurture your deepest hate.
Can you imagine?
What's your mental state?
Never again to touch,
Your true mate...
Afraid of love, won't live or date
A hundred times over
Is how a woman feels,
When she has been raped.
The uncaged animal has been released
Exploding madness of her beast,
It will take her whole life
To find internal peace!
Immortal Act...

A PART OF SOCIETY

I've searched all over
For my true love
Someone who could love me
Like no other.
I can sense his radiation,
Imagine his deep penetration
I can hardly wait for our relations.
When we're not together
I can feel his meditation,
Deep thought deliberation,
The time we've spent
Has taught me patience.
His fragrance makes me weak
So explicit, his past unique,
Every time we're near
My heart skips a beat.
People make things so perplexed
The looks they give,
Feelings reflect,
So much hate and disrespect.
Annoying harassment persistently so
Some moments I think we should let go.
This whole world is really mean
Thinking everything we do is unclean.
Is one sin greater than another?
The Bible doesn't say,
Neither out weighs the other.
Just because I'm a male who likes other males,
Doesn't mean my soul will burn in hell.
I've excepted who I am,
And burst out my shell
No, I wasn't deprived or abused,
My parents raised me well.

Gays have a right to fight
Like slaves had to do for their rights.
We are all people who are free
Just because I'm different,
I still have feelings.
If you stop judging, then you'll see
There's really no difference,
Between You and Me!

ANGEL IN DISGUISE

I was sitting on a bench
Waiting on a ride.
When some other folks came and sat beside.
They frown at a young man trying to hide.
I guess they felt high and mighty filled with pride.
We are all the same regardless of what size.
He was very heavy and dirty you see,
At this point in his life, he accepted who he would be.
He was happy and pleased because of his good deeds
A shell of a man is what they believe,
An angel sent by God they wouldn't receive.
The rust showed buried in his knees,
He said politely, might I have a seat please.
His clothes was covered in mold,
You could tell he slept, "on the streets in the cold."
His hands were welded in dirt,
His stomach hung out beneath his shirt.
No shoes or socks on his feet,
Bruised body like he had been beat.
I felt his pain with a simple stare,
Instantly, "I wanted to give all and share,"
Every bone in my body cried out of care.
The other folks decided to stand
Out of self-righteousness
They couldn't reach out their hand.
Who really has the right to judge?
What happened to realistic love?
None knows what the future holds,
Watch what you say and whom you scold.
You can't see their inner soul
You're not in control,
Gods wrath of judgment…
"Will be told."

You won't know how it will unfold.
What you think, is less than what you know?
What you see and who,
Don't always show.
Like an ever-burning light that glows.
Every second of time change the flow.
You can never predict how things will go!

ARMS OF A MAN

Holding me, while I resist your hand.
Although you're my husband, I love another man.
The reason for me staying is my kids,
My true heart I keep hid.
I have been deprived of true happiness,
This is the reason I must take my risk.
Every since your friend gave me that first kiss.
I've branded him on my forever list.
We got married for the wrong reason,
I gave you my life this is my season.
When I'm with him my soul feels risen,
But once I go home, the bars are sealed on a prison.
There I'm belittled and made to feel really low.
Freezes my love and my touch has grown cold.
Why are we going through the motions?
The person on the end
Has had to sit still and watch your bed of sin…
It will be hard for you to let me go.
As if you have feelings your willing to show
Can you imagine, my tears of rocks?
Only when I'm in your friend's arm.
Sometime I want to take that notion
And I feel in my throat an erosion.
I don't understand,
Why are we going through the motions?
My body is divided in three you see,
Truthfully you don't want me.
The person in the middle is not really I,
For a long time now you have watched me die.
The person on the end
Has had to sit still and watch your bed of sin…
It will be hard for you to let me go,
As if you have feelings your willing to show.

How many nights have you beat me in the floor?
Can you imagine my tears of rocks?
Begging and pleading for you to stop.
Only when I'm in your friend's arm,
This is the way I escape your storm.
Because a real man,
"Won't do a woman any harm!"

BAD SEED

Hidden deep under her skin,
The other person that lives within.
The side that wants to kill and hurt,
Numb to feelings, acting like a jerk.
Evil grows roots in her head,
Her ideal for peace rots on deathbeds.
When protein has separated from the blood,
Porky pine needles when she gives you hugs.
Boiling Hate fights with love.
Can you imagine whom I'm speaking of?
A spoiled rotten child
They always end up buck wild.
You only see what they show,
But those demon horns will soon grow.
Playing a baby in your face,
Scheming on when they'll take your place.
You know that child you think doesn't smoke
Is behind your back on the street selling dope.
The one who gets more calls...
Than a phone company,
Yet looking with one eye, saying
I'm doing nothing but being me,
The secret part you'll never see.
My wrong can't ever come to light,
When it does, you say that I'm right
Standing behind me ready to fight.
I tricked a lot of people,
But in there sight,
Breaking your heart to understand.
I must learn on my own,
My behavior is my biggest fan
Crippling me by your cushioning hand.
Hard life will be my last dance!

BEAUTIFUL

Your beauty is beyond pleasing,
Growing more astonishing
With every season.
A priceless ruby without reasoning
A point of reckoning,
Like the sun heat beaming,
As the dew gives into the steam
The wind tickles your perfume breeze
Faded colors of fallen leaves
Crystal frost of ice when it freeze
A priceless collective personality
Apart of sociality the world always sees
Who even could believe beauty
Further then the human eye,
You caught the glare off the flames of fire
Giving smoke a shape as it goes higher
Perfect layers flayed to a crisp
Shimmering chimes dancing in the mist
A touch as pure as a captive dream
A smile shapely defined mankind,
Can't understand what it means,
Gracefully, dazzled diamond grains
That can never fade,
I could never do nothing, but thank God
For his breath of life he gave.
Your transcending of love
And kindness on a wave.
Even death angels would fight with the grave
Just to yield you many healthy long days
Beauty like yours is not a pattern
In so many different situation
You're that ever-burning lantern,
Sensitive to other peoples' feelings,

Reaching out to help with others healing
Everything you leave has your mold
A pinch of good in their soul
But you, my dear, are so *beautiful!*

BETRAYAL

The biggest betrayal was to our race.
Once upon a time, once upon a place.
All of us weren't kidnapped,
And brought to the United States.
Some of our own people, "sold us like bait."
Now if you traced history
Back all the way through,
Some of our own people, "used us too."
You will see the real betrayed.
Of our people was, *"YOU"*
Don't blame the white man,
Because we were used
Some of our own people, "sold us like bait"
It's not one, but many, whites
Help set our ancestors free.
Open your eyes and you can't help but see.
Even to the point of teaching us to read.
The apple didn't fall far from the tree.
Although we choose
What we are willing to believe,
More than blacks were driven to their knees.
And being hung from Hickory trees.
"Cut down like falling leaves."
"Cutting off their penises."
"Stuffing it up their butts."
Yet and still blacks, "did not give up."
So before we build up a wall of resent.
Bow down, "on your knees and repent."
Then ask yourself, whom do you truly represent!

BEYOND SKIN DEEP

Further than the eyes can see
Apart from you closer to me.
The side you hate is what makes me free.
I'm better than you'll ever be,
You were born to birth evil into the world.
All around you demons swirl,
Before your sight
Blinded by Jesus light.
To show a little love for your black race.
While your living a lie
We're from the same place.
The real fight is inside of you,
Your madness can't separate the two.
Because of this you chose to choose.
Denying who you are is down right rude.
Your heart is…
Paralyzed with numbness, painless to feel.
How easy it is to lose what's real,
Apart of life motionless to feel.
Treading on thin ice could get you killed.
Without birthing the shame of your color.
You'll never truly recognize another,
"Time to stop running my brother!"

BLACK SHEEP

So far away from home,
Know there's hope and you're never alone.
All black men are special inside,
They should always keep hope and us alive.
Truly fate has stood by their side,
To survive slavery and learn to live again.
Your mind bondage has come to an end,
You've lived all your life, been told what to do
Never, ever having to choose.
Working from sun up until dusk,
Knowing you better not complain or fuss.
Living in a shack covered in rust,
Running for that dinner bell,
Hearing your master scream and yell.
No soap or water to wash off the cotton smell,
Being beat until your flesh curls up,
And that horsewhip in your skin gets stuck.
Blood rolls down your back ,
Cooling your body from the heat.
Stun and motionless you can hardly speak.
There have always been two kinds of Negroes
One on the inside and the other time has mold.
The master always had a wife,
As well as young slave for his other life.
So many old people still stuck back in the day,
Don't understand the new generation,
Can't see things our way.
A time where half their life stood still,
A moment of lost happiness and their will.
Looking in the circle it doesn't seem real,
Every time black men hear the word boy,
It takes away a peace of his joy.
Once again he's locked behind a door,

Seen as an out cast in our society.
All because blacks want to be free,
Hidden blocks of cement chain
Grinded in blood our roots and name.
The fact that things has not changed,
But Brothers hold your head up high.
Another season passed, just say goodbye,
Believe that someday we shall rise.
That day will mark all our lives!

BLEEDING HEART

One day, I was walking down the street
I broke into a sweat,
Much more than a heap
A sharp pain stabbed my chest,
Ran down my arm
Up underneath my breast
More air seemed to be less.
My life flashed before my eyes
Disembodied my spirit flies,
Looking down on myself
From the skies.
Everything you leave has your mold
Began to rewind
All my tears and fear
Caught up in my years.
So many things I failed to see
The person I judged is really me.
I can't be saved
I'm beginning to fade
Trembling with fear
I see my grave,
My family and friends
Feeling betrayed.
Moments of emptiness
Takes its toll
This is the moment
I've lost control!
Wow, shocking me down below
Who hurt me?
The paramedic working,
Not letting me just go
Who stole?
This sinful life, fighting to hold

As my body started to get cold
Then my heart began to throb
I realized it's me I've robbed.
Ever so silently my eyes flinch
Stuck motionless, my fist clenched.
Now, the last seconds,
True moments I reckon,
I see recording
Is my life aborting!

BLINDED TRUST

Here I sit tormented by life
Crying for help, seeking advice
Always pity comes at a price.
Comforted with lies on what's right.
Every night ends in a fight,
Who could have trusted this man?
My one and only mother
"That took his hand."
Pretending to be my true friend.
Day by day my boyhood is on trial.
Because of sickness
My mother can't defend me and it's allowed.
How can I grow up and be a man,
I'll forever be confused about a dress or pants.
He promised my mother
He'll take care of me,
Blinded by love she couldn't see.
That every night I was forced on my knees.
A man like this my mother can never please.
Pushing his worm in my mouth,
White stuff pouring out like a sprout.
I'm stuck here to be abused,
Bruised up rectum,
My body continually being used.
I can hardly have a bowel movement.
No pain medicines can ever sooth it,
"I go to school everyday,"
Pretending like everything's ok.
It's so hard, "at p.e. and when it's time to play."
I wish I had somewhere else to stay,
My mom doesn't even have a month
Already her life has gave up.
Every breath seems like her last,

This man she loves puts on his mask,
A secret so Hideous and cold,
I can't ever say it until I'm old.
"My joy stolen from my heart,
My mind babble to disregard,"
He looked my mother deep into her eyes
For one brief moment, he began to cry
"He promised to take care of me,"
So her soul could rest in peace.
Little did she know. "I was his feast!"
Infected by my step-daddy,
A mad, monster, beast.
If my cry for help is ever heard,
I want people to know…
Rape happens to boys just like girls.
There are so many sick people in this world.
Open your mouth it's safe to tell,
Believe in the system it will not fail.
This man that wronged you,
Should be in jail,
When judgment come,
If he doesn't repent,
He'll burn in Hell!

BLOODY HANDS

Here we are in a court system
That was designed to protect them.
I am really an innocence man,
There is no blood on my hands.
Yet and still I'm forced to take a stand.
What have they accused me of?
Nothing short, "but because I'm a thug."
All my life I've been pushed and shoved.
Don't rejects deserve a little love?
Sitting in that big black chair,
He would take my freedom
Without a thought or care.
No time for what's right or fair.
Death waits for me to share,
Justice know I won't be here,
Grave brush and comb my fear.
Who would think I could love someone so dear?
This world is not ready for a black and white couple.
We got caught in the middle of this shuffle.
Now I must face tears of crime,
As if I don't know they're lying.
This is not I
Kissed with memories of goodbye.
Dried eyes can't seem to cry,
Nothing but red roll down my face.
As I face the stupidity, "of the human race."
I'm the pixy or escape goat,
Here on my chest hope float.
How can we say we're a justice state.
When we judge people,
Sending them to the electric chair to bake.
The truth cooking on a grill, like a steak.
If you're poor or black it turns into a snake.

Money is the power everyone can see.
If you're unfortunate then you will bleed.
Nothing short of Judas seed,
When Jesus, "was sentenced to die on the cross"
For the whole world, so we wouldn't be lost.
Who will wash their hands
After my blood has been shed?
Not the justice system,
They sharpen the knife "to chop off my head!"

BIRTH CONTROL

When you reach the age of maturity
I know you're interested
In exploring your sexuality
But there's a certain degree of responsibility.
Forgive me if it sounds
Like you need your parent's permission.
What I'm trying to say,
Is you should always listen.
You're special with great potential.
There's no limit on what you can be,
Believe in yourself
Then you'll see.
Sex is not a fulfillment or a need,
Talk to your parents before you proceed.
It doesn't matter, condoms or pills
Never act to fast on what you feel.
Babies and STD are real
Are you really ready for a bone-chilling thrill?
There's Aids out now: it defiantly kills.
You don't have to play.
It's your deal.
If you think you're incomplete
Know this is obsolete
Your body is so unique,
Don't treat it like a piece of meat.
Unprotected sex could ruin your life
Every time you do
"It's a roll of the dice,"
Teenage pregnancy is no joke,
It's spreading to our young people
Faster then dope.
Stand firm there's still hope.
So many devices used to lure,

Whether its full term or premature.
Walking though this life is no tour,
You can be tricked faster then the drop of a dime.
It only takes once, a slip of the mind,
True knowledge of wisdom comes with age.
No certain point, time hasn't any stage.
So many birth defects,
Too many things that can go wrong.
It's the child that suffers,
A life outside your own

BORN ADDICTIVE

From the day I was conceived
In my mother's womb.
I knew what treatment I would receive.
Force to dance with Mr. Doom.
A so call mother that violated
And mistreated me.
Before the day I was born,
Her idea of good parenting's skill
Would be to do me harm.
Filling her body with toxicant.
Knowing it's me she's embalm.
Toss in her stomach,
A drug nest storm
In my heart a lost hides.
A hopeless chance that I'll survive.
Hello, look, I'm a failure to thrive.
From your body I must feed.
Drugs and alcohol runs through me.
Replacing the nutrition and vitamins I need
How can you think were alike,
Your habits, you chose could steal my life.
What part, "do you justify to be right"
The fact that I'm not worth the fight,
Stuck to a machine,
Under a Heating light,
Cotton taped on my eyes;
"I don't have sight."
Tubes running through my body, so I can breath.
Mother your birth to me, "was selfish indeed."
Skin so thin, you can see my bones.
Born an addict, my heart of stone.
Shaking and screaming for a hit.
Drinking milk will only make me sick.

Who, but you felt my unborn cry?
Did you even care that I could die
A innocence victim, "a pound in size."
What would it take for you to realize?
Blinders on your eyes won't let you see.
Who gives you the right to handicap me?
Your "I love you," is simply a line.
Mother your damage to me
Has left me chained to behind.
If I walk or talk, or have life beyond my own.
There's even a chance I won't get full grown.
The bond was broken when they cut me free.
Written from head to toe,
My special needs.
A product of an abusive seed.
The day you open your legs.
You know you were wrong,
Jesus has these kids,
Their never be alone.
Sex don't give you, "a right to have a child."
Smoking, getting high, doing drugs and running wild
Don't blame it on Mr. Habit,
You're the one screwing "like rabbits."
So the next man, "you're with that has an erection."
Make darn sure you both use protection.
If you think you're going to forget.
Go to the doctor
And have yourself fixed!

BROKEN CHAINS

What does it mean to hear broken chains,
This means it's time to hang up your slave name.
The sky is the limit; you have so much to gain.
Let go and keep it real, stops talking in slain
Don't lock yourself up with deep ridden hate.
This will cause nothing but pain,
Set up your goals, so you can achieve
Applying yourselves will help you believe.
We have freedom now let it ring,
Do your best and you will see
The whole world is the remedy.
Open up your mind and just receive.
Their was a time blacks wasn't allowed to even read.
Bared open for our souls to bleed,
Opportunities wait on no man
Options are open like grains of sand.
Join together, why should we continue to fight,
For we are all members wanting equal rights.
Keep hope in your dim sight,
Then you'll never stray away from the burning light.
If you limit your vision and give up,
Back to your roots you'll be stuck.
Stand like a man, you're no longer rented bucks.
Those chains and locks are covered in rust.
Pick up your feet, shake off the dust.
Different mouths may shoot spit,
But you're strong now
You've suffered the master licks.
Tear down that tree
Used to lynch!

BROKEN PIECES

Millions of pieces parts of different sizes
Over 200 thousand miles of nothing but ashes.
Scattered from state to state
Who but them gave their life for mankind fate?
Truly is it really appreciated?
Seven young lives struck down,
No one's pieces could even be found.
Over two billion dollars
Wanting to send man to mars.
Out in the orbit pass all the stars.
If you look back on our history,
In every single thing that has happened,
It was a great tragedy.
This is the only thing
That has brought unity with our people.
A burning ball of flames
Bared our seven astronauts name.
They wanted to help the human race,
But the shuttle was flushed from space.
Raging burning trails…
Stabbing pain, we again have failed.
Black mist smoke coal rolls on the wind.
Eagles wings fan, why has this happen again.
Data is not that important when you've lost
So many innocent lives.
Grave grabbing their spirit before they say goodbye.
The whole world weeps and cries,
A part of us has just died.
But we stand together as all voices raise.
God will watch over them,
Now that they are in his skies…
Our country will never erase them from our mind.
Forever treasured until the end of time!

BROKEN TRUST

We have betrayed the only one that loved man.
A king that gave everything,
And reach out his hands.
Countless times giving us a chance.
He stands for everything that's right.
"He gave his life without a fight."
He left the Holy Ghost to give us sight,
Before He rose to that bright shining light.
"Shed his blood."
Because of his love."
We have a chance to live up above.
He gave trust to Adam and Eve,
They were tricked by the devil
And their own disbelief and greed.
Now we follow after their seed,
Who are we really aiming to please?
It's not our Heavenly Father, no indeed
He hurts to see us in a struggle,
Hate on hate against our brothers.
Mother and daughter showing disrespect.
Choking the life of love from each other necks.
Father and son having sex with men.
Neighbors using the system,
To destroy each other and defend.
Children separated again and again.
"Different countries at war."
"But no one can really win."
To kill life that you can't replace, is really a sin
We toss and turn with good and evil,
Trying to hold on to our soul.
But in reality, "Jesus is the one that behold,"
He wants us to be one way,
Either hot or cold, not changing everyday

This world would buy you if your willing to sell.
But know in the end, You go straight to hell.
So, we have already broken the trust between man and God.
Stop, look, and think, "now give Jesus your Heart!"

BUYING TIME

I stop by a store called buying time.
I knew I really had a lot on my mind.
So I grabbed a basket and began to shop.
I could feel my heart wanting to stop.
It was confusing with what the store sold.
But in bold letters,
It said, "your never to young or old,"
Everything there was on sale.
But I knew I couldn't let my soul burn in Hell.
All my life I've seemed to fail,
My strength and hold on seems to always bail.
I passed by different aisle,
I force myself to give a smile.
I saw the girl that lived next door.
The one I beat up and kicked to the floor.
I said I was sorry and I'll never do it any more.
I went down a little further and passed my rent man.
The one that has the cripple hand,
He asked me for help plenty of times.
I never stop, "I just put him out my mind,"
And who can forget the homeless lady begging for food.
I spit at her, so she would move.
That dog I beat to death with a stick.
All because he licked my hand,
Every dog I see makes me sick.
The child that fell off her bike,
I laughed at her all day and night.
My mother, "I put in the nursing home,"
So I could live in her house alone,
This store held all my pain.
And on the last aisle there sat shame.
I knew without staring, "engraved was my name!"
As I walked to the counter to check out,

I saw the water of life pouring out a spout.
I said, "fill my cup,
Because I believe in something but never luck."
I stepped in the line,
I saw the most, "beautiful sign!"
It said, "Jesus forgives you all the time!"
I went in my pocket to pay,
The clerk looks at me only to say.
"Jesus is the truth and the way,
Would you like to start working for him today?"
He came to save the souls that are lost.
So to you, "my dear friend, there is no cost!"

CAST AWAY

From the time I was conceived
Until the day I was born.
I've always been sad and alone.
It's like even then my heart knew
The life of hell I would go through.
Putting me in the middle of the twins,
Sorrow and misery like I would blend.
Good and evil holding my hands,
God had my soul even then.
Abandoned as a child
Because of who I was,
Deprived of kindness and gentle love.
An innocent mind taught to hate
Prisoner of someone else's mistakes.
Mangled and confused, tied down with lost,
My self-esteem is what it cost.
All my years passed before my eyes
My family I trusted covered in lies,
Left me battered and bruised
But I survived…
True feeling and words
Sewed to my chest,
I'll take them home to Jesus
When my grave gives me rest.
Endless time could never
Clean up this tangled mess,
Mother, I know you feel
You've done the very best.
Tell me…
Where was my security nest?
Pain and confusion…
I'm compelled to confess,
I'm not like you
I've failed your tough love test!

CLASS CAME BY

Class came by to see me today
He had a few things he wanted to say.
We were talking about ugly bags,
Molded and dusty attitudes covered in rags
Laughing real hard he said, "You must be mad."
As I looked down your memory street
I was so shocked I could hardly speak.
The people that you've looked upon
Have no life and class of none,
I understand why you see past the horns
Because of their evil,
They are covered in thorns.
Although they're loud and want to be heard,
Knowing their behavior is a little absurd.
Their minds moving like a pig herd
They crave to feel your electric surge.
They can't understand what makes you free
It is Jesus Almighty they can't see.
They were born with no self-esteem
Because of this they're wrapped in mean
Dirt that can never be cleaned.
If maturity was something they could buy
I would truly recommend
A lifetime supply.
If respect didn't think they would reject
A wise idea if they met,
A touch of class is something hard to get
If you weren't raised with it
Then when it's close to you, you'll get very sick,
Like a small shoe that will never fit
Some people just weren't meant for it.
Stupidity and childishness grows deep within the bone
You don't even have to speak for it to be known,

Written all over your face it is shown.
The devil throws out his treats
You're his dog running for the meat
When he says jump, you don't ask why?
Being simple minded as you are
You say how high?
If you see yourself in any of these lines,
Then stop listen and read the signs.
Class is something you've never had
Be mad with yourself
Because, Honey, you are sad!

CLOSE YOUR BLINDS

When the thunder rumbles deep in you,
And you feel like what's before you is disgusting.
Even if it's not blocking your view,
Razor hair grows on your back.
Then you're harassed without any slack,
Waiting in the dark to bash their heads.
The near sight of them makes you mad.
A thousand times over you wish them dead.
Do you know whom I'm talking about?
More then half of the people at dinner,
It's them they discuss.
When in reality,
It's your envy that's about to bust
Gay bashing is so meaningless and cruel.
For there's only one Jesus and he rules.
Who really can cast stones?
Outcastes making them feel alone.
This world is our entire home,
Sin is flesh attached to everyone's bone.
Jesus said, "the greatest of all things is love."
Do you have any to speak of?
To push someone to an early grave,
Because they didn't flow on your wave.
Shooting arrows of words,
Won't make them straight.
Even after death they'll still be gay.
Only Jesus can show them the way.
Do you beat down and abused people who drink?
Have you ever looked closely at yourself
Without a blink
You're perfect, meaning with no fault.
Is this really what you think?
There's no spots or sin

It's only Jesus that can cleanse.
Lying, getting high on drugs, fornicating
Adultery, hanging in clubs
Does this make you a lesser candidate for love?
Sin is sin in God's eye from above,
Gays have been around since
"There were Kings and Queens."
In front of our faces yet unseen
Doesn't mean they should be viewed as unclean?
The average wife lives on her knees.
There are not many lines,
She won't cross
To keep her husband pleased.
"Jesus is the only true judge!"
So the next time you want to frown.
Stop extend your arms with love.
We all do wrong,
Like day change to night.
Every second we can't live right.
Now if you think gays, "put red hate in your eyes."
Jesus made them with lids.
"Close your blinds!"
No one should be forced to live a lie.
We are who we are
SO WHY DENY!

CLOUDS

Puff of softness
Pillows of care
High in the sky floats on air.
Depends on the weather
Cloudy or fair
They never disappear
Always there:
Apart of natures beauty sheer.
In prison purity locked so high,
So close to the sun, yet won't fry,
How can you describe such a remarkable scene?
Yet in the open, but bare so clean,
Above all of us with no selfish means.
Grayish mist the air needs,
It's like it's stuck it never leaves.
On our atmosphere it feeds.
Fluffiness we don't understand.
Never once touched by hands.
Expletively so no one truly knows
Why clouds have an endless glow
That moves across the sky
Like a river flows!

COLOR BLIND

We are living in *"I have a dream,"*
That remarkable speech,
That was given by *Martin Luther King*
"He saw a future that no one had seen,"
Black and white together as one…
Every time they saw police,
"They didn't have to run,"
We're an interracially couple.
Who has survived the American shuffle?
There are no more slaves,
But in people's minds.
Some are still trapped in those days.
Mankind just can't change their ways.
It was hard for him to find a job.
They watched him like he was the mob.
We couldn't even find a place to rent.
They wouldn't say, "what was wrong,"
But they gave allot of hints.
Sometimes we pointed it out.
Their response was that's not what we meant.
Love is supposed to be blind to color,
How is it we can't love one another?
Hidden scars on his skin,
Where he's been lynched by so many men.
"Stuffing his balls in his mouth!"
Reminding him, *BOY*, you're still in the south.
Their insensitivity said you'll never be free.
I fight everyday so he won't leave,
When will the madness stop
So the love of my life can breathe!

THE CROSS OVER

Here I lay filled with fear
Now that I know my time is near.
Even if this is my death walk alone,
I'll turn back time
To make this place my home.
My spirit has locked to my body you see
Afraid to raise, fly high, and free.
Oh, please! Death Angel pardon me
Show a drop of pity and mercy.
I know I put my life in a mess
Ignoring rules knowing it wasn't for the best,
Revolving chain around my health
Now look at the hand I've been dealt.
A losing battle I fight to win
Even though my time is near an end
I hold tight hanging by a strand
Will to live, please hold my hand
Grab health to fill me up
Sickness stings my heart is stuck
There is no such thing as luck
It's only the wraft of God
My will is lost in this thick mist of fog
I see a light on the other side
This is my hope and my guide
Slay of Spirits let me hide
You don't have to take me
On that death ride,
I need peace and another chance
Please, let me do that victory dance!

DEAD MAN WALKING

A rotting corpse still walking around
You don't understand
Why you're not in the ground.
Maggots are crawling all about
Over a million deaths
Now you've lost count.
You're thinking deep in your mind,
Why am I still living?
Endless time...
Without forgiving.
You smell the rotting of your flesh
It's decaying away
Soon there will be nothing left.
Yet ...
You won't die
You ask for mercy
In every tear you cry.
Tired, but forced to go on
Like an old record
With a never ending song.
You see the devil's wolves
Biting at your feet
With teeth of pain,
Gums dripping black blood
Every drop burns your name.
Claws of steel surrounded with flames
You're still standing, begging
Let me be...
I'm not the bad one
It's my flesh, why won't you see?
You think back on all the things
You've done and said
Remembering the pain you inflected,

Forever your burning bed.
This is your life without Jesus Christ
A billion times over,
This is the price.
Repent for his love understands
With flesh there's sin
But Jesus is your faithful friend.
Confess with your mouth
Take his hand
Do you not see without Christ?
You are a walking dead man!

DEAD SILENCE

Who would know the secrets I hold?
Around my friends, ever so cold
Moment of truth can never be told.
My innocence abruptly stolen,
So much pain my insides are swollen.
A child trapped in a palm trade,
Used up body, strangers love slave.
I was broken in young, starting as a babe.
From my brothers, and his friends,
All kinds of grown different men.
My daddy, I must confess
Treated me like the rest,
He used to say I was a princess.
Mother doesn't understand and can't see.
That which she knows and won't believe.
She hates me, thinking I took her place,
A ripped body, a child's face.
It burns so bad when I urine,
I can't control my bowels
My body's ruined.
They climbed on me to do their business.
I block the whole world out and refuse to listen.
Stabling pain runs all the way through,
But I stay strong and try not to move.
After a while my body goes numb,
From head to toe my body is stunned.
When I think it's over here comes another one.
An old fart tender feast,
Lock in a cage with a leash,
Burned rage, covered grief,
Young life, almost deceased
God, knows my disease.
Only in rape is there peace,

Immature mind can't compete.
"Bleeding heart stony deep!"

DEATH BY TEMPTATION

What is it? To want love so bad
Subject yourself to misguided madness
Body floods with torment and sadness
Hungry for that treat,
You couldn't get enough
For years stringing you alone
To kill you she must
Blinded by your lust....
Poisoned fruit between her legs
An old man like you she has enslaved
She's irresistible, her body you craved
A molded pet she has made,
No sleepless night
For the way she behaved.
Before you drown in your last breath
Realizing she stole your health
Never did she love you only your wealth
You're surrounded, frozen with blackness,
One step from death
It took your life to see what she felt.
Terror and hate both had your fate
It was her riding you as you masturbate
Horror deceived you with a face
Her secret lover that took your place
Spoon-fed poison
Until your throat closed and you couldn't speak
Kindness, love, and trust made you weak
Now your body suffers defeat
The devil's puppet has not been beat
Forever you lay in this motionless sleep
Father know her day will come
This is the beginning for me,
Believe it, she has not won.

The entrapment that caught you
Can't catch me
I'll never stop, 'til she's brought to her knees.
Before the world, her evil will be seen
Admitting her plans
And dirty schemes.
So, even though death claimed you
Too late to be saved,
Holding justice sealed in your grave,
The beast that wronged you
Someday she'll pay!

DEATH ROW

Here I sit waiting for my day of execution
The ending of my life, final conclusion
Like the front lines of war,
But without the revolution.
I can feel my body joining with death
Mentally, I'm prepared,
My heart has dealt with the emotions I felt
Cold-blooded cruelty I refused to melt.
My mind rewinds the retrospect
Every single aspect
The fact still remains,
I'm the third generation of rejects
All I wanted was a little respect
Blinded injustice made me the prime suspect
To help some senate get re-elect.
The perpetrator is the one the system protects
I have no regrets,
And sympathy hasn't called
What silent peace behind these cement walls
Dangling meat for wolves and dogs.
If you understand then you can hear
I separated my soul from that tormented fear
The deceased provoked my anger combustion
Now, I must suffer the repercussion.
Innocence looks guilty before the human eyes
Every heart hides the truth from lies.
Who among us has the right to judge?
What happened to a brother's love?
In this event the 12 jurors were wrong
The judge still passed down the verdict song
Given purity a form,
Confront death torture alarm.
Yes, I resent your judgment!

When you sentence to death
A man that's innocent!

DISCOURAGED WOMEN

I've opened my ears to you
And I've heard your cry for help
No need to worry, let Jesus order your steps,
Your depression is heart felt.
The beauty in you can't be put into words
Find your strength, let it emerge.
Your body is precious, keep it sterile
Don't prostitute yourself
You are worth unspeakable wealth.
I know you feel you need this
But you're opening yourself to many risks
Why be a victim to loneliness?
The things you can catch has an endless list.
Some reach out for the poison
Because they're homeless
Believe me my child you are blessed
Put your life in God's hands,
He'll handle the rest
Know in your heart
He knows what's best
The devil is pushing you,
It's just a test.
You're a descendant of a King
Value yourself by all means
Do you know what prostitution really means?
Just a deceitful way pimps say
She's not clean.
Ask yourself this,
What have I missed?
What happens when your goods fade?
Six to ten years just waiting on *AIDS*
They've used your body, like you were a slave
You have nothing, but their house is laid

You're not even good enough to be their maid
Now can you see who's been played?
Look what your body went through
All the torture and abuse,
Still walking the streets for days
Don't you know there's another way?
Through faith everything will work out, *OK!*
You're special inside, there's no doubt
Do you understand what life's about?
There's so much more,
It's your choice.
Don't walk through that door of pain
Smothered in shame
Afraid for people to know
Your real name.
If you believe in yourself
There is nothing you can't gain!

DISEASE YOU WON'T WIN

Ms. Multiple Sclerosis is not my real friend
She reaches out to hold up health,
As if I wouldn't understand
Like masturbation of my own mind
I'm doing the encouraging every single time.
I refuse to give life up and die
I'm determined, "to win and I'll tell you why."
Muscles and Nerves have put up their sign,
But my heart is strong and the will is all mine.
Nothing can bleed my soul you see,
I will be faithful to every part of me.
I see Illness making his rounds,
But I have decided I'm standing my ground.
And though I seem to lose some weight.
I'm still not at Grave's open gate.
It's my belief that controls my fate.
What I give and what I'm willing to take.
Who says I have to participate?
This bed throws webs on me,
Don't want me loose or free,
But it's Will that will never leave.
I'm only sick if I believe,
Bedsores stop by my room;
Said he'll see me very soon.
Baths and massages on a daily basis.
I won't run, and I will face this
There is no way Bed Sores is coming this way
Everyday I feel strong and there is no horseplay
I'm being rotated from side to side,
Mr. Pneumonia you better hide.
I'm deliberately being stubborn with my body.
I will make this my daily hobby
There is no way sickness will rob me.

A cure will come,
Multiple Sclerosis can't help but see
One day soon I will break free.
"I'll never give up hope
On what I believe,
I'll keep on praying"
Jesus will pick me up off my knees!

DIVORCE

Across the table
Sits the woman I once knew
In spite of our differences
And what we been through
The fact remains, I still love you
So many moments, I want to turn back
All my dirty secrets, I hid in a sack
While reaching for
My gentlemen suit of the rack
I never tricked you in your view
Even behind your back
You knew every move,
You stuck with me win or lose
I drove tacks in you, covered with blues
You honored and admired,
Showing nothing but respect
That piece of paper was permanent,
To me in the beginning,
She was an on call Whore for rent
I greatly apologize and repent
You were the best thing in my life,
Truly heaven sent,
I can only cherish all my mistakes
My abuse has taken over with fate
As I look in your face, I see true vows
You're a special women with your own style
Holding your head up so proud
Who can save me from myself?
Now that the real me was allowed
I've murdered my own life and lost this trial
All because I wanted to taste the call of the wild
What is really left now?
Me giving off that stink, smelling foul

So I sign the paper now letting you go
But there's one thing, I want you to know
My feeling for you
Will never demolish, they will grow!

DRUGS

Let me break it down for you
Even though I've never walked
In your shoes
I can see clearer, so here's the news.
Drugs will only set you back
Don't think for one second
The cops will give you slack,
Living in darkness nesting like bats
Running scared, imitating rats
People walk all over you
There's no respect,
Change your name to welcome doormat.
Different hospitals are there
To help you get off drugs
Support groups around you
To extend their love.
Millions of heartbreaking, sad cases
No certain colors
All races from different places
Addiction has many faces.
Look through my eyes
To see yourself,
I hope you understand
With Drugs this is all
That can be left…
It takes you to a make believe world
Man or Woman, Boy or Girl.
It helps you run from your problems
An endless road never going anywhere
When you come off your high
Guess what? Your situation is still there.
It blinds you, so you can't see
Think hard and twice,

It will land you in jail
For the rest of your life.
Drugs can steal
What little you have left,
Why would you want to rob yourself?
When you're used up penniless, broke
Lost your friends and your folks
You gave up all this just for dope
A brainless, longhead
Spreading the plague
They're getting rich
You're on your deathbed.
Your teeth are rotting and falling out
Your vocal cords are gone
You can't scream or shout.
The taste of feces glued to your tongue
Your body's in shock,
Your mind's numb,
You're crawling on your knees
Scraping together crumbs
Now, you see Drugs spell out dumb.
There's nothing left but a shell of waste
You're then ready for a resting-place.
You could never give your blood to anyone
No matter how hard you try,
Hang up the madness, there's no way you can lie.
From head to toe
Drugs always show
People won't say, but believe me they know.
Every high puts you at risk with AIDS;
Run from your master
Why be a slave?
There are two doors you can go through
One can save or the other...
Opens your GRAVE!

ENVY

The knife in my back watching me bleed
All the torturing pain brings me to my knees
There you sit watching, waiting to feed
Over my grave your rotted wreath
Rejoicing because I'm deceased
You've locked peace, never to be release
In my heart the beast marks you
Who could have known what you would do
Hidden hate rips my bones
Riding behind me, won't leave me alone
Where is your right that blinds your wrong?
Hunting me down, sliced by the pound
Nowhere to hide sniffed out like a hound
Even death can't be my safety,
While I'm in the ground.
A texture so smooth, waiting to decay
Pigments show your color to betray
We survived our difference, like night and day
What do you serve to justify your way?
Your impression was designed to kill
Gluing your mind, intention, and will
My joy and happiness you would steal
Now this corpse can never heal
I plead for kindness; you spit pus in my eye
The numbness of nasty, prevent me from a clean cry
Pinned to the wall I ask myself why
Your jealous greed would see me die
All your words were crocheted lies
My spirit of goodness will still rise
A recipe for your internal demons seed
Living in a pouch, wanting to breed
Deprived because of the beauty in me
Covered in waste, you can't see

Because of your black cold heart, you're never be free
Forever haunted by me, who you wanted to be!

EVIL HAS A FACE

Two eyes, one mouth and one nose
An obsessed mind
With a heart that's frozen cold
Morally bad and out of control
Vicious intentions,
Rude with different moves
No help for others, following no rules
Thief of life, crushing eternal peace
Satan is their daddy,
Taking the mark of the beast
Indirect consumption of reading between lines
Illusions optimistic,
Has already twisted faded time
Who could have such a free will?
To brutalize, torch and kill
Souls' chipped hardest steel,
Are you,
To care what others feel…
A panic on a rotted corpse,
Easily maneuvered, eagerly envy aborts
A partial blockage shield by fear
Evil that's so silent its pure…
Dripping with filth smelling so foul
Face motionless, eyes of an owl
Horns and blood stained teeth,
Hidden animal from the wild,
Evil has a face and it comes from one place
Lost heart, covered in waste
Picking, smiling every single day
The cruelty of mankind, apart of the human race!

EXECUTION OF THE TRUTH

The Jackal spreads the word
Trying to reach out to the world,
Twisting what we know to be the truth
Putting you on the spot, so you must choose,
Carrying a bible in his hands
Coming off like he's your friend.
His first agenda is to win your trust,
While he's watching your wife and daughters
Dripping in lust,
Then he isolates you,
Making you part of his group
Telling you he's your father
And you're his troop,
Now your family
Is one of his many chosen recruits.
Here you have sold your home
To join a cause rotten to the bone.
He sends you out to work in the fields,
While raging on your wife and kids at his will.
They know better than to resist,
Without touching them
He has twisted their wrist.
Nothing to eat or drink,
Pushing for you to change your ways,
Locking them up for days
Because some won't be his love slave.
They're forced to eat their excrement,
And some bite their extremities...
In a tiny small box stuck on their knees.
Licking the excreta that they catch with their hands
Taking a moment
To think where their faith stands.
These people are searching for the world

Having sex with sisters and brothers, boys and girls.
Taking your mind apart piece by piece
Robbing you of ever having relief
Working for your food from dawn till dust
Throughout the whole church building
Is the smell of demon lust.
Sin took a form and it bared his name
A sound mind now drenched in pain.
They will kill you and any other that comes around,
Blinded by their truth, the devil's trumpet sounds
Nothing but pleasure to put someone down.
Cult is not a mist,
Just like the sun and moon
It truly does exist.
This is not a story people want to be told
It goes against everything we hold
True and dear in our soul
No one has the right
To have that much control
Read the bible for yourself
So you will know!

FAMILY BURDEN

How much can one family go through?
All we're doing is what Jesus tell us to,
We run out of food with nothing to eat.
My dad worries and hardly gets sleep.
Daddy works overtime everyday,
And is too tired when he comes home to play.
Our bills are behind,
Where is the money going to come from,
I can hear Jesus say keep your eyes on me.
Cause I'm the one,
Although I'm young, I know how to pray
I believe in my heart Jesus will make away
We're lucky to have a roof over our heads.
So although I don't have a lot,
I love Jesus too much to get mad.
So many bad things I've seen in my young life.
But I've never doubted Jesus once or twice.
At Christmas when kids are happy to get a tree.
I think to myself, I'm happy that Jesus set us free.
I don't wear nice clothes to school,
They pick on me, but I think they are rude.
Because I'm serving Jesus, "I know I won't lose,"
See, "my Lord knows what is best,"
I just have to be patient and wait on the rest
Even Jesus went through a test,
So if I fail, I'll get up again and again
Because in my heart I know,
My family burdens can't win.
And on Jesus' word, I can depend!

FAMILY SECRETS

Smothered in the walls of this house
My father, the Rev., being the boss
Painted over so no one can see
Is the cult that has blinded me?
Practice to do evil, rather then good
Teaching to hate, as if I would
I come against him all the time.
Telling myself where to draw the line
My dad has five wives,
And all he does is bathe in lies.
When he plunges in me, "it feels like knives,"
Stiff as a board, all I do is cry
He takes turns with us
As I lay, "covered in spit on dust,"
In Daddy's eyes, I see the lust
My mother is one,
My sisters and brother are the other four
Long ago, "we should have walked out that door."
Who would have known?
My dad would choose the wrong side.
Letting Satan's demons be his guide,
Day in and out he puts us down,
Striping our goodness off by the pound.
He thinks he's building,
"A kings tower, working us every single hour,"
But really deep within he's turned sour.
The devil gives off wacky power,
I take risks every time I pray
Because I'm asking Jesus
To guard my spirit while I lay.
Although the poison is taken in my lungs
I know this world can't do me harm.
The devil is tricky,

He'll even give you your needs.
But I won't be fooled, like my mother *EVE*
The Holy Sprit is what I will receive
And I'll forever stay on my Knees!

FLOWER BED

Out front for the world to see
The best in everything there can be
Beauty beyond any dream
If there is faults it can't be seen
Surrounded with miss perfect
And miss lean
Always on your knees
Picking the weeds
I can never grow
To make you happy or pleased
You can't see my life
It's your prison of needs
Faultless vessel just for show
If there was ever love
I would never know
Everyday your passion
For control would grow
Painfully rooted nice and slow
Water down the truth, you can't let go
Desire confronts me with a tormented alarm
The fact remains you will do me harm
Accepting fear dries up my tears
Time don't exist in passing years
Covered in the soil of Mother Nature
My heart wasn't given to you,
It was taken
All around my world is shaken
Never will I grow to be free
Every time I sprout
You cut a piece of me
Killing the tree
So I can never leave
Rooted forever to pay
For your deeds!

FLOWERS OF LOVE

Some say you can tell how a person feels
By the flowers they like
This may even determined their insight
If they are a wolf and how fast they will fight
If they're a koala bear that holds on tight
Red roses may mean they're easy to fall in love
Yellow rose could say
They're distant with kissing and hugs
And brightness sparks their heart to floods
But they shine, like a 100watt bulb
Tulips bring tears of joy
Maybe you've given up or want to challenge the score
Sunflowers and daisies have always been friends
If you received one of these,
You will truly know where you stand
And really feel safe to shake their hands
Violets rapacity of most women's hearts
Trembling her soul, every single part
Johnny Jump Ups are every kid's dream
You'll never see the real child,
Because they're so gentle and clean
Who can let go of Poison Ivy?
Just itching in your pants,
With a whole rotten mouth of cavities
Every woman wants a pet,
So she can let him out to play
Nothing like a big kitty to watch you in the day
Then the dandelion at night
Holding her feathery tight
There we come to Miss Venus Fly Trap
Women watch out, if she gets that man on her lap
A trip to the doctor can only help
So men don't loose that belt

Cactus is just in for the long haul
Don't wait by the phone, cause he won't call
It would take a lifetime to get him up
By then ladies cobwebs will be stuck
Who would think to leave out weeds?
Every household has them
Even if they can't be seen
Those hang up calls and slow drive-bys
Women you already know your man is telling lies
Men and women run from fungus
If you're always opening
Your legs, that's the big risk
Please, don't go with that first kiss
The next thing you know, you're on herpes list!

FORGIVE MY HEART

Have you ever stopped
And really stood still,
Your heart explodes
With pain freezing chills.
Have you ever felt something
Almost too good to be real
In one brief second
Life is being murdered
Forgiveness has been killed,
Sickness creeps in and steals,
So filled with sunlight
Strength fights to heal,
Even if it's a short moments give.
You'll sell life's gift for the right to live
While death rolls out a mile long will
Then the truth opens and reveals
You shuffled this hand to deal.
In a fraction of a second, you lost control
Treasures tricked you
Now, what do you hold?
Secrets no one in this world could know
A stiff cold body forces out his soul.
Your heart bleeds hidden drops of gold
True emotions come unfold
Your womb coming open, deep and wide,
What you once had is the only guide
Unwilling heart
Soaked with too much pride
Now, you see your other side.
Teach me to say goodbye
Honesty hits me in my eyes
Hateful and mean
Left me twice,

Filled to the rim
With kindness and nice
Lord, let me come in your paradise!

FOUR WALLS

Serving time for what I have done,
A battle for my life has just begun.
I'm stuck doing twenty to life,
The only one can save me is Jesus Christ.
I'm not perfect, I made a mistake
These four walls have sealed my fate.
You have to be a man in here,
Standing firm and clear with no fear.
If it must come down,
I'll fight until death.
There is no such thing
As taking care of your health.
Men get beat and raped all the time.
From every color and every kind,
Once you cross that line.
This is a world of its own
You must be tough and strong.
We have our own rules,
The weak get played as fools.
Speak up in order for you to survive.
Day by day corpses come by
No time to weep or cry.
And you must tell the truth
Don't get caught in a lie,
Or your butt will be set on fire.
The officers' turn their heads.
They don't listen to anything that's said,
You have to break your own bread.
Behind these walls is a touch of hell,
Even the food taste bad and have a stinky smell.
Hunted by the thing they call it,
Burns when you use the bathroom,
And hurt when you sit.

Prison is a place nobody wants to go,
Everyday could be your last
Even windup being someone's whore.
Night after night you lay in your cell,
The walls and bars whisper,
About the mausoleum they call jail.
So if you have any intention of breaking the laws.
"Think again, brother,"
You don't want these four walls!

FUNERAL

Well we are here
The place where the dead sleep
Corpses have no fear.
Rotting on the end is near.
The doors open wide
A usher on each side
So many sad faces,
And not one dry eye.
Men wanting to be strong,
Yet, "even they break down and cry."
Time is short,
I didn't have a moment to say goodbye.
Just thinking,
All those times hiding behind lies.
I'm being carried,
In front of the church.
As my body rolls pass
I can feel so much hurt,
They open the casket
Finally, I'm well rested.
It's going to be hard
For them to get pass this.
Here I see myself,
I can't imagine how they felt
Unbearable pain, as they wept.
Burning like a rotisserie deep within them,
Come to a boil when they hear the hymn.
As I'm rolled back through those doors.
Sorrows vibrating the floor.
I can sense the fresh grass,
Realizing now, I can't run "at last!"
I've made roots with my pass.
Now they lower me in the ground,

The seconds of stillness sound.
Death hugs the dirt dropping on my grave.
I'm glad in my heart I've been saved,
This body scared, but my soul is brave.
There I was at the ending,
Nothing else that really needs mending.
God rain showers has holy powers
A way of releasing the dead
"Through living flowers!"

GIVE ME MY FLOWER

Here we are, I'm sick as can be
Half way blind and can hardly see
The deeds I've done, I don't regret
All my life, I've showed nothing but respect
Who will cry for me when I'm gone?
Having left this world all alone
Tell me where's my next home?
A place where you can't visit me
Away from everything even the sea
Flying high with the birds and bees
No more body, sick and diseased
Jesus will have set me free,
Only then will I receive flowers from you?
There's no way I will know, not even a clue.
The spiritual world holding me like glue
Look at you, putting flowers on my grave
Why didn't you give them to me in my living days?
As if I could smell their sweetness
Or even know how much I'm missed
Feel the petals giving me a kiss
What are you thinking?
I'm on the decay list
Beside my corpse there's a group of friends
Rotting and hollow holding my hands
Bitter and Stink saying they understand
They live in the ground, just to watch man
Resisting defeat until the bitter end
If I could turn back time and start again
How many flowers would you send?

GIVE THANKS

Heavenly father,
So full of grace.
Thank you, Jesus
For taking our place.
Bless this food
We're about to receive.
Thank you, Jesus
For supplying,
All our needs.
Amen!

GRANDMOTHER

How can sweetness be put into words?
Like the fresh air, floats the birds
The rotation that spins the earth
A bust of power when a tornado twirls
My Grandmother, my one and only girl.
See growing up was hard for me
I was stubborn, doing selfish deeds
My Grandmother stayed on her knees
Interceding her plea,
Lord, protect her, please!
My head was hard, mind blocked
Didn't want to listen,
Queen of my flock
Insane madness never wanting to stop.
My Grandmother knew
I couldn't see clear
Never once did she show any fear.
Jesus' voice from heaven
Is all she could hear?
Constantly telling me,
I love you, dear…
Now that I'm grown
My grandmother has gotten old,
She still shines, her heart of gold
Deep in her soul, my story is told.
Granny can't do,
A lot of things for herself
Thoughts and emotions
She's placed on a shelf,
Incurable aging, decaying health
I'll take care of her
With every breath.
Granny saw the good in me

In spite of all my mistakes
Granny is the sweet in sugar,
The moistness in cakes.
Forever, past eternity
My Grandmother
I'll always appreciate!

GREED

So spineless, inconsiderate, and cruel
Greedy, thoughtless, and down-right rude
Always trying to use people,
But you're playing yourself for a fool.
The people you're trying to starve,
Someday they may have to help you.
What you fight so hard to hold,
The day will come and you will lose.
How can you feel good about yourself,
Not caring how others felt?
No one's responsible for the hand they're dealt,
But you can open your heart
And pocket to help.
So many people you have not paid
Yet you betrayed your kind
Both our ancestors were slaves.
You forgot who you were,
How the way was paved,
Who suffered and the sacrifices
They made
You, I'm happy to show,
How low you will go.
You'll scrape the milk off the tongue
Of a sucking infant babe,
Even your maids don't get paid.
On the streets
You're known to be cheap,
You'll beat down a dog
Just to take its meat,
Finding enjoyment
Out of the children you cheat.
Even the homeless would never get a dish
If a man like you had his wish,

When you go down, you'll remember this.
You cut every penny,
Dice every dime,
Believe me my brother
You'll get yours in time.
It's happening right now,
But you don't see the sign;
Justice will judge very swiftly
Everyone of your kind!

GOD'S EYE

There is nowhere you can hide
Even when you're on God's side.
He sees your high and lows,
No matter how far you go.
Going to church twice a week,
And in between you're running around to cheat.
Stand up shouting for joy,
Then passing yourself, around like you're a toy.
Why would you treat your body like a whore?
It's you that God adores,
Of course men will find you to be a bore.
Giving church members a ride.
Then afterwards,
Gossiping with tongues of knives,
Preacher shaking your right hand.
While his left eye winks and dances,
So many members know what's in his pants.
Going out to witness,
Then add them on your return list.
Sealing it with a Hell Fire kiss.
Something in Bible study you truly missed.
Singing in the choir,
Crying "Lord, take me higher"
Then on Saturday night, looking for a buyer
Going to rehabilitation homes,
Talking to crack heads and drug addicts.
Then sitting on the toilet, getting you a fix.
Asking the drunker," not to drink"
Gods' "watching and he won't blink"
Praying with all your might,
Then on Thursday through Saturday.
Hung over with your pint,
We wear one coat that's nice and clean.

Yet, "there's dirt that can't be seen"
So before you pull out your brother's splinter.
Thinking you're so spotless and clean,
Look close in the mirror,
And pull out your own beam.
Know you're being watched "by God's eye"
Watch it, brothers and sisters, that's living a lie!

HARMONY MY PEOPLE

So many years ago
Knocking on freedoms door
Slavery took its toll.
Even now a part of our heart
Bleeds cold.
Burnt down deep it has left a mold
No consultation could ever console
Open your mind purge your soul.
This kind of grief will consume you,
As death has shown.
Never think that hope is gone
In time destiny
Will give us our home
Until then, we need to get along.
Kids coming up today
Race is not pure
They see a different light,
One free and clear
No colors, hate, or fear,
They'll only judge
On the things they hear.
So join each other in harmony
Come together
With the song of peace
At some point the anger will be ceased,
This is the time when healing is released.
Rejoice because we are free,
Our biggest generations today
Are minorities?
They will soon control our society
A memo for our future,
They are the majority!

HAVE YOU NO SHAME

A big country with justice and peace
But truly how long is our leash
Our constitution defends everyone's rights
So where are the teeth?
How hard is the bite?
Let's take a closer look; shining the light
Putting to death people, we put through the system
What if they're apart and we truly miss them
The real soul deep inside,
Whom the human eyes can't see.
Dry tears don't mean they're a lie
In their hearts, they could really want to die
Who defends and takes their side?
What defines a mental blow?
That stinks your mind and ability real low
Who's to say how far to go?
Criminally insane or to slow
Who started and set the flow?
Does anybody truly know?
To decide guilt or innocence
Isn't how they are represented?
But to take it further and put them to death
Now two families are beat with whips
Let's just walk through how they felt…
To put on a diaper to catch their waste
Acid urine and running paste
Eyes taped so they will stay in place
Justice and judge have spit in their face
Watching for the color of their corpse
Their body jerking, shaking, and then barf
Bodies covering crisp, fried, burnt skin
As the grave embrace a newfound friend
Who really can judge their sin?

If you weren't there how can you swear
There's always doubt, if it's just a hair
Take a moment learn to care
Know whose heart really laid bare
Can you honestly say that's fair?
Do you even dare?
Whose shame bares a name
What is it you hope to gain?
Putting another life through all that pain
Have you Sir or Madam any *SHAME!*

HEAVENLY FATHER'S GRACE

Anytime you sit down to eat,
You should thank our Heavenly Father
With your eternal soul of meek.
He loves you beyond any measure
Our mind can't understand, God's pleasure.
He gave his only begotten son,
An unimaginable treasure.
Don't you know you owe.
"Him your life?"
There's none to live
Without Jesus Christ.
The Father, Son, Holy Sprit is one.
Accept his hand and your battle
Is already won.
So the next time you sit
In front of your plate…
Don't forget to say,
"Our Heavenly Father's grace!"

HEAVEN SENT

To all the women missing fruit and can't bare.
Here's a miracle, "I want to share,"
Take a moment to feel my care,
Growing up as a child
I've always had a practical style.
Never did I get real wild,
I was smothered and covered in nothing but love.
I've always believe in the Lord up above.
As I grew up my body began to change.
Later a special man gave me his name.
Nothing in my life has been the same.
Thirsting for joy and happiness,
I put my man second on the list.
We had Jesus and each other,
But somehow we were missing one other.
We wanted to make our life complete,
So we decided to have a baby
With two small hands and little feet.
However my sadness rapes my peace,
I had been barren by a disease.
But see the God I serve,
He's king of everything.
In and above this world,
He created the universe in that great big sky.
So, I would never dare to ask my God why.
I know because of my faith
My needs and desires he will supply.
I want to see life pass my own,
Joined together to the bone.
Setting free a part of me,
Someday will be when I leave.
Reflections shining bright and pure as a running stream.
Without a wrinkle or spot-free, snow white clean

Doctors said it could never be done,
But our battle has already been won.
In my womb the seed had begun.
There is only one that can give life.
And his name is Jesus Christ
What he does is out of love,
My baby, "was always in that cradle up above!"
So, I know my child is heaven sent.
God doesn't make mistakes,
She was definitely meant.
So for all those who feel like your lost.
Accept Jesus at no cost,
He makes the impossible, possible
Before your eyes.
Give him your hand and be mesmerized!

HELL RAISER

Words carving envy in me
Spiting and cursing,
To the point it burns and stings
Aching deep in me.
Like a thousand bees' stings
Your heart of frost bite,
A touch of freeze,
A mouth that's uncontrollable
Exploding in its need,
Just like a junkie with a habit to feed
How can hate become a person,
No such thing as peace or fun
Even the grass fear your feet
By clearing a path to run,
Air gets permission before your breath leaves
You're feeling like a less soul,
That's hard to please
The fragrance off you
Kills flowers, plants, and leaves
Sweat of acid causing you pain
Low self-esteem baring your name
Our relationship was finagle
Which explain why I'm living this hell
Gentleness or kindnesses always fail
A house with you is a rotting jail
Pinned to the wall in a vomit cell
Nothing I do will make you happy
It's time to let go, so I can be free
Your air of pollution paralyze me
I can't breath, only in separation
Will I get relief, other than that?
It's rather I am deceased!

HIDDEN HATRED

One voice started a long time ago
Deep down south where the rivers run low.
A voice teaching them it's ok to hate,
That the reason for blacks,
Was God made a mistake.
He started a group
They called Ku Klux Klan
Pledges to never ever touch a nigger hand.
They said their living the bible
And their ways are true.
If this was a bible of God
Then they would love you.
Their hobbies was to kill at will,
They felt it was no reason for blacks to live.
Not one minute of peace
They were willing to give.
Their parties were to catch a nigger.
By their necks, "they would hang."
Malicious and vicious describe their names,
Cutting off body parts horrible unspeakable pain.
The words they said was offensive,
But their whole flock laughed and listened.
Everyone was apart of this group,
Judges and policemen were all brother-hooded troops.
Branded in their heads,
Was a rope of thirteen knots above a loop?
Blacks will keep extending their hands
May someday we'll live in peace
On God's beautiful land
Side by side all colors will stand
It's sad the brotherhood has transcended up to this day.
They still believe blacks should be slaves.
Never can admit they were wrong,

Or change their ways.
The brotherhood will take their hate to the grave.
Now those blacks are free and can read,
The Klan hate is hidden, so it can't be seen.
But it still shines through like a lighting beam.
Is it really that hard for mankind to see
That we all started with one seed
And believe it or not
"It started when God created Adam and Eve!"

HOLOCAUST

An invitation to meet death
Little time to think about yourself
Every moment is focused on your family that's left
Tearing us apart as our heart weep
Fear burns with every step
Here they place the weak in a line
Who but us would want to kill time?
Standing, shaking, losing our mind
Hugging and telling
Each other everything will be fine
We face evil chin to chin
Only on prayer can we hope to win
Our pain and torment now begins
Pulling our loved ones to the other side
The children are afraid and try to hide
We take off our clothes in disbelief
Raped with fear and lots of grief
Knowing we are apart of the deceased
Simply because their ruler was stamped by the beast
Those that wasn't shot or hung
The shower of gas burst their lungs
Holding their breath until their chest swells up
Tears runs from their eyes
And in their nose ice of blood is stuffed
Ending is their heart in shock
Then it's over, their organs have popped
At that point they wait on them to rot
All their bodies piled on top
Worn wrinkled, scared hands tied in knots
Apart of their soul still trapped
But it didn't take long for them to adapted
Between the beatings, kicks, and slaps
Starvation because of the shortage of food

Working in the cold with no socks or shoes
They are free, but we should see
That every candle light burns and freeze
A pain buried deep in their sleeves
Branded on their arms for the world to read
Jews hunger for justice and a life of peace
The ones who wronged them are the diseases
And someday, they will be brought to their knees!

HOUSE OF PAIN

As I stand over this cliff
My body frozen stiff.
Reminisce on the fun days we had
And now how my life is so sad.
My heart is in turmoil,
Beating my head against this wall.
As bloody drops began to fall
In spite of our fights with the racism.
This mean cruel world has imprisoned.
I refuse to deny what I know to be true.
There's nothing I want more,
Than to be with you,
The hate they harbor,
Is like a tumor that grows.
It went on so long
Until now it's out of control.
My life shields you, because my love is known.
I know this is right,
Yet, "I'm fighting with your wrong."
Our souls are magnetic,
Every since the first day we met.
You've always showed nothing but respect.
Like a bodyguard, that protect
All these walls bleed your name.
Buried alive in this house of pain.
The floor has gave away to say,
Join him, today is the day.
That brings me to the point, "of where I am."
Tugging at my feet, the limbs
Holding my body up is the wind
Birds chirp encouragement
Trying to make me strong again.
Jesus whispers, "this is a sin"
I lost the start and hugged the end!

HOUSE OF STONES

This whole world, is a house of pain
So many things we need to reframe,
Why do we associate white as good?
And black as being bad and out the hood
People refer to black as being a Negro
Or our people are ignorant or slow
White people are intelligent and smart
Everyone assumes that from the very start
God created all of man,
Regardless of the color of his hand
You can't tell where they stand
Who is the isolator of what is in their head
What they been through,
And how it should be read
Jesus wants all of us,
To join together and break bread
So if you took a magnifying glass,
To dissect your pass,
Following every single trace
Searching deep at every place,
The one you're looking down on,
As if that person is toxic waste
Really once their revealed
It's your bone structure
And a true reflection of your face.
So the next time you
Want to put down your own or another race
Repent for your fall from grace
Jesus died for one and all,
So listen to the blood call
Black is a shining bright
White is a shunt of sight
Airborne is freedom and equality rights

Give to each other,
Love with all your might,
Turn this hate of black
To a white, black raining, rising light
Because both are needed to win this fight!

HUMANE

It's time to forgive, unite and live
We don't have to see each others color
It's just a matter of what we will.
How much are we willing to give?
Search your soul and I know you'll feel
The earth is dying
We need to be real
Ask yourself what can I give?
We can change,
No need to kill
Adore each other
We're sisters and brothers?
This planet we abide on
Is our mother?
We should take care of her
Better than any other.
This is all our home can't you see
We hurt ourselves by cutting down trees
They give us the oxygen
We need to breathe
Every part of them we need
Even down to the fallen leaves.
Bushes, dirt, grass and weeds
Polluted waters, oceans and seas.
Save our planet, why don't you please?
Our ozone layer is burning fast
When it's gone
How long do you think we'll last?
All creatures, every mammal,
Let's not omit one single animal.
A 100% of man creation is flammable
Now tell me again who should be liable…
God put us on this beautiful planet

This is not justifiable.
Mist of fogs, drenched in smog
Mobs of gas…
Soon we'll need masks.
Mankind can't outlast this
Our whole generation is at risk
Then we sit back and wonder
Why so many people get sick.
Don't you know?
Were on the verge of being *extinct*
Read the signs: catch a hint…
Earthquakes, erosions, volcanoes exploding
We can stop anytime
Our core is unfolding.
If ever I needed people
To get the urge,
Listen closely to my words
Feel the surge.
Let's come together
To save our world!

HUNGER

Love is a word
You shouldn't throw around
But you're used to
Sluts and high whores in town,
You're a dog
Your breed is a bloodhound...
That nose of yours
Could smell manure by the pound
Running your game
Trying to tear me down
What do you think this is?
I'm not your clown.
All your lines are broken cries
Your thoughts are empty,
Full of feelings you fought to hide
I'm so glad, we've said goodbyes
That tongue in your mouth
Is covered in lies.
Respect, you can never earn
Do me a favor keep your germs
I survived this lesson
Believe me I've learned.
I made a mistake
My nerves you no longer shake,
Your heart of stone will soon break
Giving birth to your pillow of hate.
I won't be used or mentally abused
This is my life,
And you will lose!

I CAN'T FORGET YOU

I can never forget you, even if I tried
I feel your breath when I look at the sky
To say I could, would only be a lie.
All the waterfalls coming from my eyes.
You are my everything
I would never say goodbye
Without you I couldn't live
I would surely die.
A love that's pure and clear,
At night you're the voice I hear
When I need comfort, your always near
In spite of my ways, you are there to count on every day.
Although I fall a lot, you tell me everything's ok.
You never have to be ask,
For you to show you care.
I never have far to look, for you are always there…
All my problems you share,
When things get rough and I want to give in.
You're the strength in me, so I can win.
I'll never worry, because on you I can depend.
When I'm puzzled, the right words you'll send.
Your kiss is like the blow of the wind.
My heart, body, mind and soul,
Only you will forever control…
You're the peace in my life that unfolds.
The only one who truly knows,
Written on me from head to toe.
You're name that's whiter then the driven snow
"JESUS, JESUS, JESUS, I'll never let you go!"

IDENTITY

God gives every one characteristics,
Which puts most people, "on the defense list?"
When you're being real you're at risk.
There are different manners,
"Based on the way they are raised."
A brewing stew makes them misbehave.
It's hard to contain.
When measures and performance steps in,
With deeds and you'll trail as if your win.
We are all unique in our special way
The weather changes people frame of mind,
Just like the days.
The blow of the breeze,
The coldness that freeze,
Cries out to the humans,
Actions, "which is the disease."
There is a rage in every one's heart that grows.
No one can view, "who truly will know."
A trigger that put your being on trail.
Were all apart, "of the call of the wild."
Hidden deep within is that child voice we send.
Trembling on the fringe,
But a camouflage, "so we will blend."
Who can break the beryl?
Of the nature that we see,
No one but God,
"Because He created you and me!"

IF I COULD SPEAK

Here I am new to the world
Am I a boy or a girl?
My body feels slimy and wet
Look how they scrub me
Do they think I'm a pet ?
They introduce me to Mom
We've already met
For nine months she carried me
I think I know her scent
What is that bag
With one big eye?
Every time I grump or cry
She sticks it in my mouth,
Singing a lullaby.
It's nice and sweet
It makes me feel strong,
In a few months
I'll milk it on my own.
It's hard to see
Except in front of me,
People are talking all around
They look so funny.
Faces like clowns
I can't understand
So I laugh and frown.
Nothing to do
But eat, sleep, poop and play
There's only one thing
I truly can say,
I'm in Mom's arms
This is where I'm going to stay!

I HAVE A CHOICE

A loaded gun pressed against my chest
Cowardly, I face an easy rest
A cry for help at mercies best
Pouring stress, loving a lot less
Anger clinches the trigger
Voices grow,
Rather it's a wiggler or nigger
Brutal truth,
Life itself is the dealer.
Rich or poor,
Reality holds no pillows
Gangster styles,
Cradle for the wild
Lost, confused, stone-cold child;
Truth or Dare
Came to share
Crowd of uselessness,
Accompanied with despair
Cheering in my head,
While they sit and stare
If you even knew,
No way you would care.
Down in my world
Every man for himself
We're killing each other off
Soon nothing will be left
Our offspring don't think,
They just yield
Fog of darkness,
No emotions to feel
It's your stigma that has molded this will
Lessons burn, but short time lived
A mirror can only reflect,

The monster in you, you've feared
Death loves this, your soul it steals
Low self-esteem, madness reveals
The you inside wanted to shield
Violent fight with control
It's your mind
Give in, or learn how to survive!

I KEEP SILENT

Behind these walls
Bloody teardrops began to fall
All this time in my parent's house
You can hear the footsteps of a mouse.
I Keep Silent!
For years my mother beat me, you see,
The only peace I cried out to be free
I was mistreated for so long
I had no love for myself,
Respect of care gone.
I Keep Silent!
Although I love her so,
Every word from Mom's mouth
Tears me down low
Like kindle
Above a fire real slow
The scorched, burnt
Heart in me would grow
The shame I hide
No one could ever know.
I Keep Silent!
My innocence
Gave my mother power,
My craving for love
She used to devour,
Moments I trust
Drowned me in lying showers.
I Keep Silent!
Now that I'm grown
With a life of my own,
Feelings covered in smirks
The need to live alone
I forgave the moments

Of hard times I've been shown
The mother that stands before me...
Reflections gone
Because of who I am now
My eyes will no longer shine.
I Keep Silent!

INCURABLE

Hello, Dr. Fatal and Mrs. Grave
How are you doing today?
What brings you by to see me?
Did you know Critical and Untreatable?
Won't let me be.
Dr. Fatal and Mrs. Grave
What is it you have to say,
Well, Tomb and Vault wanted to stay.
In here with me, "there is simply no way."
The head of this death ward, Mr. Grim
He makes the decisions talk to him,
I wiped the slobber from my mouth,
Thumped Mr. Heart, "in my bodies house"
I said to him, "Jesus don't move on doubt!"
Pried myself from the bed,
Trembling and shaking halfway dead.
Mr. Lethal, I don't need a shot,
What is Morphing doing?
Trying to make my Heart stop
Or better yet sending, "my Body into shock,"
Miss Burial Place left me a note
I guess, life threatening to beat up hope.
Dr. Fatal wants to keep me doped.
But nothing can separate my Spirit from Mr. Float
Spirit will fly to Heaven to talk with my father.
I know he loves me and it's no bother.
He'll heal me, "with a wave of his hand!"
I'll stand and shout doing the Holy-Ghost dance.
Listening to His angels band,
Because Jesus has saved this sinner-man!

INNOCENCE

Girls and Boys save your virginity
It's the key to your purity,
Waiting is the secret to your maturity
Life's innocence will form your personalities.
Youth will wait to mold your old age
Moving too fast is a price to pay
Mistakes reach for your hand
Itching burns deep in your pants
Your mind only thinks it's ready for romance.
Then it's your moment alone
Both of your parents are far from home
Your face is flushed,
Your blood rush,
Believe me, my teens, it's simply lust
Remember that your bodies are precious.
See, so many boys and girls,
Just waiting to devour and use
They're running a game,
Guess on who? You.
Your innocence is very special,
And when the time is right,
Then you'll choose.
If you're pressured into intercourse, then you lose.
Growing up takes guidance and skills.
Rushing into sex is a matter of will
I know you think the fact of life is no big deal,
And this is your body, you'll do what you feel.
Sexually Transmitted Diseases are real,
And AIDS don't have a cure pill.
It doesn't just make you ill
AIDS chokes your life and kills.
Take your time, wait on what's right
You deserve the best,
You're worth the fight.

INNOCENT UNTO DEATH

How can I pay for a crime "I didn't commit?"
How is their justice?
When it's the truth they resent,
I have the courage to stand strong.
Even if I'm in this alone
How can I go down for killing myself?
Instead of judging, get me some help.
I'm not pretending to be insane,
I really hear echoes of my name
Telling me all kinds of bad things.
I sometimes want to hang,
This torching blister pain.
I've killed my whole family
My wife and kids a part of me.
Blinded by greed and lust,
The pain in my heart is ready to bust.
That inner being robs my pride,
Won't someone please be on my side.
This hidden rage, "I fought to hide,"
I've lost my mind and standing still is time.
The other side turned sweetness to bitter.
It's like I blinked and He hit her,
Everything was over before I realize.
Who would have knew the heart of me just died,
Every beauty in me from the inside.
Under my surface there are two faces,
When I do evil he trade places.
How can you punish me as if we are one?
When really the other is the smoking gun.
I am innocent and he is guilty
One body and two personalities…
Only when I'm bad can the other be seen.
So why can't he wear the death ring.

I'm innocent; "I didn't do anything,"
Won't someone simply "please speak for me!"

INTERNALLY ME

I see this person who feeds off me
Oddly so with curiosity
A complex puzzle no one understands.
Prison of mirrors come and go with life spans
Who's there to catch me when I fall?
Heart of glass, no mouth to call,
Under my feet, giving away is earth
Burning deep to become my hearse
Cleverly of death is not the first
To surround my body,
With the stricken of hurt,
My shaken soul toxin wastes
Glued truth, dripping paste.
Blistered tongue numb to taste
Hidden beauty molds to my face.
It's only a tic before the hour,
Forced erection, explosion of power.
Sitting is sin, waiting to devourer
Hatred has a mountain of nerves,
Who can judge on what I deserve?
My life, my choice
Death shock, electric surge!

IN THE CLOSET

I'm raised in a home
Where I'm lost and so very alone
My parents don't want me to be different
Because of who they represent
They see me, but only in their way
I'm forced to hide my secrets everyday
Running after a rolling dice
Who decides on what is right?
If I come out, there will be a price
I stand a good chance of losing my life
Outcast forever is the way I would be
They're so blind and refuse to see
I must be honest with myself
In order to be free
My tears are like the running sea
All night and day,
My feelings sting like bees
Can't ever feel love, because of who I am
My future is blink and all so dim
In my head a burning ball flame
I have to lose what could I gain
Fear and will shout my name
Dipping in colorful shame
No one can imagine this unbearable pain
My inside has turns against my body
Searching my soul for a hobby
As my boyhood wants to leave
Watching the real me bleed
Inside of me a lame dead horse
Will anyone listen to my small voice?
This is my body; it should be my choice
I don't want to be straight, so why I'm I forced
I'm a boy who's an individual

Why should I have to listen to mental blows?
Everyone has a sin only Jesus knows
Let me come out and show
Roads are endless let me grow!

INVISIBLE PAIN

As I walk down the streets
Big smile on my face
They can't see my defeat
That lonely rat race,
All this time living alone
Matters…no opinion it's all my own
To hear my pain
You must be deaf
The mirror of shame
Fills my empty shelf
I wrapped myself in emotions
So fake
Running scared from my mistakes
Afraid of sin
Wanting to be free
Selfish judging, ridiculing me
My mirrored reflection
Screams, let it be,
Shelterless, Homeless
Waiting on fate
Still smiling, but trembling
I'll never break.

IN YOUR SHOES

Pattern in my mother shoes
Watching her get high and drink booze
Trapped in a triangle of I must choose
Fighting the battle I may lose
Who can save her from herself?
Don't care about life and no one else
All these different men in and out
It's like my mother has her own route
How can I learn to care?
If my own mother is never there
A battle that's not yet my own
A war right here in my home
So many years before I'm grown
When it comes to living right, I'm all alone
Molding me to do what's wrong
Needles fill with pain and shame
Hitting her arm to find her vein
A ragging animal that can't be tame
Why did her beauty fade?
She looks three times her age
My mom faced Mr. Failure
Prostituting herself with her seller
Looking at the truth is a big dip
Now she realize she's slip
Every high, takes her on a make believe trip
Once she comes down and looks in my eyes
Heart of stone too stubborn to cry
Caught in a whirlwind of lies
The scars on my skin,
Is nothing short, but my mother sin?
Who gets buried in the end?
All these footprints my mom has set
Nothing to help shield me or protect

If I fit them, then I lose respect
Someday when I'm older
I'll search for another size
At that point, I'll say my goodbyes!

I'M TAKEN

When I hear your deep voice
It still rumbles my soul,
Selfish love I fight to hold.
I'm Taken!
Those sky blue eyes cry out to me
Dreams of what
I wish could be,
I hear your heart beat
Say please.... Don't you see,
I'm Taken!
The truth before you is deceived,
Stuck in your throat
Can't you leave?
I'm Taken!
In your mind
You've said goodbye,
Stabbing me countless times
With your lies.
I'm Taken!
Broken, motionless, frozen cold
This is not the way fairy tales are told.
Bleached smells
Cover your dark black soul.
I'm Taken!
Craving to feel on my cheeks
Your lips that are so moist
Desire me,
Drawn together by a magnetic force.
I'm Taken!
Looking in your face
Blinded to you, Humbled truth…
Denying all your moves.
Must I give up this race?

Maybe we'll meet
Another world beyond space
This time is not our moment or place.
I'm Taken!

I'M THANKFUL

If your eyes fail to see
The joy that I'm thankful lives in me.
Just in case you don't know
The inner part of which I am must show.
Flesh of sin I'll soon let go,
I don't need it in heavens door.
It's only caused mistakes down here below.
I've suffered so much in these young years.
A mountain of tissue wouldn't dry my tears.
Uncontrollable rage fights my fears.
My love for Jesus always yields,
His unconditional love He freely gives,
Surrounding me with his anointed shield.
This whole world can't hold His will,
Jesus covers me; He's all I feel.
The love for Jesus is so great,
Life treasures could never out weigh.
In my heart Jesus will stay,
No matter what fight I face everyday.
I may not know the time
Or the way.
But because of whom He is...
I know everything is already ok.
Jesus can never make a mistake,
A mustard seed of faith is all it takes.
He's in no hurry, but He's never late.
"Just be thankful with patience and wait!"

IT'S YOUR LOVE

Every time I do something wrong
And I began to think hope is gone,
In my secret closet I feel so alone
My burdens are heavy
My heart feels like a stone
It's your love!
Evil spirits trying to come
In my blessed home,
I fight hard and stand strong
Reminiscing on your anointed song
Burnt in my chest
From the day I was born
It's your love!
You grew in me
Like wheat grows on a farm
Never letting me stay
Far from your arms
When I feel a threat of harm
You surround me,
Like the mist with dawn
I know no tighter bond
It's your love!
Though I don't always abide
I can't recall you ever leaving my side
Your holy book my eternal guide
At moments I lose my way
You show me the signs
When I'm too slow, You fall behind
Though loved by billions
You're still mine.
It's your love!
In the midnight hours of my restless sleep
With demons riding, my spirit won't give me peace

Your strength is needed to beat the beast
It's your love that gives me release.
You died on the cross to set me free
Your precious blood runs through me
The winds whisper *I am He!*
Forever you'll supply my needs...
It's your love!

I'VE HAD BETTER DAYS

I've always been smothered in love
My life has been full of kisses and hugs,
Who but Jesus from up above
Shares his grace and mercy
Surrounding me with his angel's doves.
Now touching my prime
My number is called
From the keeper of time,
This is a test,
Who but He knows what's best
No regrets, madness or rage
Because I know Jesus I'm not afraid
My times of silent will give me rest
I feel myself dying.
There's no use in denying
I've had better days
The gates of suffering at my door
I'm not afraid I see heaven's shore,
In my heart it's Jesus I adore
My bleeding heart holds true to the core.
This cross of pain I truly bare
My bitter cup no one can share,
But my reason for pressing is not my own
My time has come; I must go home
I've Had Better Days!
My sickness robs me of my limbs
The light in my eyes grows all so dim,
But I keep my mind on Him
Jesus will never fill my cup pass the brim.
So many days and nights,
Spent in this hospital bed
Thoughts of my life pictured in my head.
I dare not ask why? Although, I don't understand

But Jesus will never release my hand
I'm facing torment and grief,
But I stand like a man
Life choking my body
Please loved ones don't cry for me
Here I'm kissed by my grave.
Every breath runs from me
I've bared my soul now I'm free
The real disease the world can't see.
Suffering and me share apart
My point of healing was in my heart.
Even as my hour is near
My voice shouts out with cheer.
All these years I've hurt and suffered
Finally my cry is heard
He's removed me from this sinful world
There is no better day then today
I'm happy Jesus had his way,
This endless moment I give praise…
Welcome, Lord,
I'm finally saved!

JESUS THANKS

It would take forever for me to say,
Thank you Jesus in every way.
So many times you have brighten up my day.
Watching over me as I lay.
When I was hungry you supplied my food.
When I was lost you showed me what to do.
Everything, that I have received in my life.
You gave to me freely, "without a price."
When I needed a hug, I could feel you there.
Every second of my life, I know you care.
When my burdens was too heavy.
You held me up so I could see.
But my side, you would never leave.
There were hills that seemed like mountains.
Spiritual thirsty for your fountain,
Jesus you floated me on your wind.
Every breath of my life on you depend
Thank you, Jesus, for being my true friend.
When my body of flesh began to fail,
There was only you Jesus I could tell,
Your hands of healing that you held.
You poured from head to toe
Then I watched that wellness began to flow.
Thank you, Jesus, cause only you know.
I'm so content because you won't let me go.
I thirst for you more and more,
When I was in jail locked up,
Thoughts and bars was sealed shut,
My sadness never went unheard,
You uncaged me like your free birds.
I fell short and my knees got burned.
"Repent and try again,"
Taking with me lessons I learned.

There's not enough time or seasons in a year.
To tell you thank you Jesus,
"Just for being here!"

JUSTICE WILL PREVAIL

If the Declaration of Independence really stood for me.
Then all black people would have equal opportunities
And if the Constitution really up held my rights.
My black leaders wouldn't have to fight.
Real life before your sight you fail to see,
Someday African Americans will be free.
The shackles are broken,
But the chain is still on our necks.
There is no justice, until we get our respect.
Some judge mental whites may say.
Its ignorant to keep this up,
Now if you survived what we did;
I know you would be nuts,
A sound mind frame on *"We Shall Overcome"*
Believe me, my brother, the battle has just begun.
Yes, Brother, it's what I said…
A day will come when we all will break bread.
Don't always follow other people,
God gave you a head…
Look through my eyes to see your hate,
No time to lose, one moment before your mental break.
We were kidnapped and brought to the United States.
Now you see you've made a mistake,
Your apologies are just too late
You can't control us now; this is fate
We do welcome you to participate,
Then you'll learn how to appreciate.
Strong and powerful spells our nationality.
We will never stop until we get fair liberty.
There's no animosity towards your race,
Until everyone acknowledge what took place.
Voices of remembrance will be in your face.
You have a few blacks you put on top,

But it's obvious they are lost...
You know like we know
They are following your flock.
Why not paint their skin
While they listen to hard rock,
Our cry for freedom will never stop.
These Uncle Tom Negroes don't represent us.
They're good for one thing,
Kissing white leaders butts.
So don't cover up and pacify,
Time to be real with your lies.
The day will come,
When our freedom, equalization shall raise.
On that great day,
We will say our goodbyes.
For all our people that hung, suffered and died.
This will mark a change in all our lives!
Your hearts will be ripped,
From side to side.
"The book of hate..."
You fought to hide!

KEEP IT REAL

What is it about our people being misled?
Broken communication in their heads,
We'd rather have name brand clothes instead of bread
Our kids walking around crying to be feed.
Sleeping on the floor,
Because we don't have furniture or beds.
Keep It Real!
What is the real difference?
Between TOMMY HILFIGER and FUBU
What does it matter;
That one is made by us and the other by you
They are priced basically the same,
Why are they throwing stones at each other's name?
Keep It Real!
AERO POSTALE, POCO and BOSS,
They're all the same, every piece costs.
See, our people want to dress in nothing but the best.
But our children go to school
And can't pass a simple test.
Dressed in all name brands and nothing less
Their home is infested with insects
Rodents, roaches and other pests.
Keep It Real!
Moms and Dads dressed to kill,
Yet, they have no working skills
Most of their clothes come from five finger deals
Do you think it's ok to buy things hot or to steal?
Some of you won't even pay your child support
Using welfare and the system to extort.
And here's the government,
Giving you a home in the projects.
You're walking around demanding respect.
Throwing house parties and cook-outs with all your friends

Cruising the town in your Benz,
With dope to sell and money to lend
Brothers, you've enslaved your own men.
Time to stop, my people, and start again.
If we don't care about ourselves,
Then neither will anyone else
We have to take the first step.
In order for us to heal
It starts within us,
Keep it real!

KILLER OF YOUR SEED

Letting the beast in your heart.
The rage of hate from the start.
Every time you close your eyes,
The spirit of that child cries.
Asking you why she had to die.
Further more, telling you you're a lie.
Pale blue face, purple lips,
Listening to her blood drip.
All because for one moment you flipped
If you were insane, "you would kill yourself."
There's nothing wrong with asking for help
When you steal a child's life,
Without doubt or thinking twice.
You live in a prison of guilt,
Every peaceful moment
From your heart has been ripped.
Your own body rejects you,
Cause your conscious mind
Knew what you were going to do.
Ardent and unmoved,
Because your soul will never be soothe.
Obsessive yet unconcerned
It's no wonder why each inch of your mind burns.
A zealous hold has made you unable to learn.
You're even unsympathetic,
Foaming from the mouth
Like a dog bit by a rabies rabbit.
Circumstances didn't hold you up
To justify what you have did
You knew all the time.
The true motive would be hid.
What mercy should we have?
You're the one who gave that child a bath.

A rag of hate and jealousy,
Tub filled with embalming fluid,
Only you can see.
Leathered up with I want to kill,
Drops of kisses the only reason is your will.
Rinsing them off with acid of death.
Knowing when you finish, a corpse is left.
Cradling them like a nursery basket,
Drying them off with Flowers and a casket.
Handing them to the grave to close the lid.
True intentions, "of a low-down *PIG*!"
Trying to stand and look like you're lost.
So many people bitten by your frost.
Faithful "to the end of what it would cost."
Your internal hell, caged with free.
Remembering your sin,
Is your revelry!

LABEL ME NOT

Why is it every white man or woman
Has wronged you?
Nothing we say makes you happy
And nothing we do.
You feel like we are so wrong
And you are so right,
But look through a white person eyes
To get your sight.
We all don't think blacks are ignorant
It's just your attitude and how you represent.
Yes, we're sorry
For all the black men and women that were lynched,
But my people have already repent.
So, why do you still resent?
It's not the fact that your color is well done;
Daily my people run to the sun.
Society shows favor to your kind
I don't feel we should make up for lost time.
There is nowhere in the world
Where you can't find an equality sign,
All generations are joined at the mind.
You need to come to reality
Stop using lines, claiming you're left behind.
Minorities have a entire industry
And you're still saying, "SET US FREE!"
So, I dare you think all my people have put you down
When there's special treatment for you all around.
What had happened all those years ago,
You need to walk through this new age door
There is no way to even the score.
How long do we have to fluff your pillow,
And sweep your dirt off the floor?
I thought you should know there's

Good and bad of all kinds,
Its your black people that draw the line.
We white people discriminate against ourselves,
Poor white trash and people with no wealth
Then look at the hungry white people
Fighting for food stamps and help,
They have to go through the same steps,
But does your heart melt?
So, believe me when I say I know how it felt.
How soon do your people forget?
Who was it that set you free?
It was white people just like me
We wear braids sometimes like you
So don't hate me cause my eyes are blue
They make contacts so yours can be too
I can't help that I have long soft hair,
Put a relaxer in yours and some tender loving care.
Why are you trying to hate 'cause we may date a black
        man?
No envy in my heart if a white one give you their hand.
There now, that we've gone through
This whole chain of nonsense
The fact is I don't give hints.
So, if you're real with good intentions
Here's my friendship if I failed to mention
Stop all this hate and tension
No need to pick a race
Just like we're here and you're there,
God could have traded our place
Then would you have the same look on your face?
I don't think so!
Heal, live and let go.
Now, the next time
You want to put a label on my head
Because your ancestors
Were buried in a slave bed
Take a moment to think,
'Cause you are being mislead

These are my views and how I feel
Although you judge, I love you still!

LAST WORDS

Once upon a time
There was a couple, who fought all the time,
They change on each other like bells chime.
Both were young and in their prime.
Forever they would live in their minds.
So many hard and cruel words
They would say,
Nothing kind not even one day.
She left for work early one morning,
An hour later the phone rang
The voice on the other end said…
I'm Mr. Death and your wife is dead.
Every bad and awful word he had ever said
Ran through his heart and aching head
All those times he wasted getting mad.
Cheating, hitting, treating her so bad.
Not one good time,
Could he think of that they had.
Who's the keeper of his madness,
While his bodies corroded with sadness.
Even though, she never said what she should.
Nevertheless, her action wasn't that good,
But you were left here to slobber
Every painful memory is a bother.
So many blunders in your life,
Now on your shoulders a mountain of strife.
Stone cold stiff she laid,
Words of knives met her in the grave.
Mr. Forgive You wouldn't even stay,
Who's going to dissolve this bill or pay,
"If you don't have nothing good to say,"
There's a bill for caring how others feel.
Watching your mouth, cause words could kill.

Negative lips should be sealed
The fact of the matter,
Is the real deal...
Respect is hard; "it has to be your own will!"

LIFE IN THE BLOOD

There is life from the point you conceive
Every thing you eat,
Down to the air you breathe.
I know you find this hard to believe
But take a moment to think,
Look closely and don't blink,
When that egg and semen connects,
There's a life you must respect
Maybe you can't see it with the human eyes
Or hear that baby laughs or cries
Ask yourself how and why
Your gift is your blood flow
If it were not alive, then it wouldn't grow
It's just a matter of time before you know
And then you will begin to show,
To take and abort your own seed
Yes, it's your body; you can do what you please
But what if in the beginning of Adam and Eve
She plucked us out like weeds
Then don't you know we wouldn't be?
None of this would exist, don't you see
So why would you act like a rabid beast?
Who will cry for you when you're deceased?
Jesus gave life to us all
How dare you take it
It don't matter how small,
And if you are raped, I feel your pain
There is help and you're not the blame
The man that did this should burn in flames
But that life is special
You have so much to gain
Someone else can give
The baby their name

There are always options, even adoption
Now if it's a medical reason,
Don't think twice,
Because by all means do save your life
But if it's because you lay up and open your legs
It's your fault the mistake was made
There is birth control,
There's no excuse for the way you behaved
So don't flush that child,
To his or her unwanted grave!

LIPS OF PRAISE

Every single time you open your mouth
You should lift your sisters and brothers up,
Without a thought or doubt.
Giving everyone love is what it should be about.
Negativity is not the right route.
It doesn't matter if it's your child,
You should always sound like you're proud.
No matter how bad it is,
Remember no one's perfect keep it real.
We're going to make mistakes,
As long as we live.
Time will move on like a turning wheel.
Our chain reaction should be passion.
Passed down a common attraction.
No one has the right to freeze someone's mind.
Hateful stuck and welded in time,
Once bad words have fallen it can't be rewind.
A cheerful word can brighten someone's day.
It's a light that will show the way.
We should always be on guard,
For what we might say.
The adversity is busy working on your tongue.
Summit to Jesus and the battle is halfway won.
Even visions that dances in your head.
The fact your body craves to be fed.
Nothing but peace and happiness,
Sealed with a stone cold kiss.
Praises is what you really should miss.
So make a note for a positive list.
If you're ever around someone that put you down.
Then these are people, "you don't need around!"

LITTLE GIRL FLY AWAY

I see myself years from now
Body used up, spirit shot down
The only joy I've even known,
Is believing someday I will be gone.
Then I'll fly high away from this home,
Burden ridden grief
I'm left to fight alone.
Raped on a daily bases
So many uncles, brothers
Forever changing faces.
Who will cry for me?
My own mother refuses see
While lying to herself
Accusing and blaming me
So she don't have to leave.
Why can't she understand?
Dad won't let me be
The only comfort
Is knowing I'll someday fly free.
I lay every night pretending to be sleep
Praying I will find some peace,
I wish this madness would cease
My own daddy possessed by the beast.
I pretend like I'm not there
This helps me to feel like I don't care.
Although the pain is too much to bear
My grave rakes through my hair.
Once upon a time
I was a baby listening to lullabies
Now, all this time I'm waiting to die
I have no tears left to cry;
Constantly, I ask myself why
One day soon I'll say goodbye.

To that scared little girl spun in lies
The reflections of my innocence won't hide,
The fear of life will learn to rise!

LIVING MUTE AND DEAF

I was born without hearing and a voice,
I don't even know the word noise.
Dead silence has always been my friend.
I talk to him many times a days,
People just don't understand my ways.
There's a miscommunication on our waves.
Although, I can't hear and have no voice
The sounds in my head are really hoarse
I'm not dumb, I still understand.
What I'm feeling inside and through people's hands.
I hear the most beautiful music in my heart.
Plays all through me every single part.
I see birds, but can't hear their sounds
The mist of nothing all around.
To want to speak grows in my throat
Just to say something to different folks.
People look at me, feeling sorry,
I don't even know why they bother.
I can laugh at my own jokes,
My endless peace surviving on hope.
I'm in a mausoleum made of glass,
Never to disagree and joyous happiness will last.
I can see the dirt and the grass
There's not too much that can make me sad.
I feel the wind as it touch my skin
The hair on my arm stands up again and again.
The birds look at me and wave goodbye.
Trees hover over me so high,
The clouds move to follow me
The sun blinds my eyes, so it's hard to see.
Animals come to me, but I'm not afraid.
I watch them move alone and they begin to fade.
Looking at other people when they dance,

I can tell by their faces if they're a friend.
For the rest of my life,
I'll never speak or hear sounds
But I must say, "it is peace all around"
Because of this, I'll never hold my head down!

LOOKING GLASS

Looking in the mirror
I could hardly recognize myself,
I'm skin and bones
With deteriorating health.
Physically I have to be fit
Even at the price of being sick.
Fashion defines the beauty of a woman
It started way back before the Romans
Being thin as weeds
No thighs or legs, only your knees.
My true relation is self-starvation,
Mental abuse and human mutilation
Stomach churning for food,
But I'm 85 pounds with ten more to lose
I'm not crazy or confused
Too weak to work
I've set my goal, no time to hurt
Living on caffeine pills
Blurred vision and it's hard to heal,
But this is my right as well as my will.
Do you really think being lean
Is going to make you a model or a queen?
The picture in that glass,
Time is short and that person won't last.
If you look close
Then you'll see who's the host.
This is an illness and you need help
People care and there are places
To walk you through the steps.
This is a psychological disharmony,
The fight is food against your body.
Anorexia is a disease that will wipe you out
Don't underestimate, there is no doubt.

A person is not defined
By what's seen by the eyes
Beauty goes deep below the skin,
It's on the inside.
A disorder like this can only lead to death
You have to take good care of you
And love yourself.
Jesus died on the cross to give you life
There is nothing in this world worth that price
Ask for help, welcome the advice!

LOST CHILDREN

No one can save me from my life
Here I'm trapped, tied to strife
Never have I listened to others advice
There's no memory of anything nice.
Coming from a poor broken family
In our house, no such word as peace,
The gang is my outlet for release
The rage I've been taught
Beats that hidden beast,
When in reality it's really me.
How can I have hope?
I feel lost and so alone
Once again the gang is my home.
Pain and deception is all I've known
I was raised to believe
I'll never have anything of my own.
In my heart I play
Over and over my hate song
Never will I escape.
Where I'm really from
There is no cradle for support,
You stare real hard at your results
Knowing your means was to distort,
My gang of youths
Will hold down our fort.
See, death is our best friend,
Living the street life you have to stand
If not, they don't see the man.
I'm not a child
It's too late for me to reach out my hand,
Let me show you your dance.
Gangs are a way for you to hide
Hope laughs at you 'cause fear is your guide.

Don't hide your shame
It's okay to cry…
There are places that will help you
People care, they're on your side.
Trust is your crutch, now open your eyes
Gangs spell out lies
Not to mention,
They steal lives.
There is no such word as goodbye
Only but one way out is to die
Ask yourself, is it worth it?
Why?
No one blames anyone who tries.
Be real with yourself,
Swallow your pride!

MARRIAGE

The first day of the rest of your life,
You must be sure you don't want to do it twice.
A million years couldn't describe what you feel.
Your decision is not your own opinion,
You have to yield,
As you walk down that aisle,
Dressed in your own style.
Escorted by your dear dad, he's so proud.
Finally peace has been allowed,
Here beside you the man of your dreams.
He's there to support you and supply your needs.
Some of your wants and desires,
This man sets your heart on fire.
You're no longer Mom and Dad's little girl.
You're all grown now in this great big world.
What is a marriage but a pledge,
A legal document to take you to bed.
Your support system only your dad had.
To share your times of sadness and when you're mad.
Two hands to scratch your itchy back,
To reach for your tall racks....
He will work hard night and days
And you already know you'll get your way.
But what other man could tell what you like.
Bring his teeth down on you,
Yet, "he won't bite!"
With just one look you won the fight.
You fell for him that Nov on a full moon.
Then you married him the month of June.
On your honeymoon, you hibernated in your room.
Already you've adapted to his tune.
This is a marriage that will survive,
There will never be any wet eyes

And nightmares of midnight cries.
Long as you yield to each other lives.
"No such word as goodbye!"

MIDNIGHT

At the stroke of midnight
When the moon glistens,
Tossing and turning because something is missing.
You went to bed without saying your prayers
Now at your foot are demons from Hell,
Witches and goblins casting spells.
A thought that never entered your head,
A battle for your soul inside your bed
The Holy Spirit from which you fled
Because of your sin and what you've said.
All day long you were playing church,
Winking and kissing being a flirt
Never gave a thought to any of your words,
So many hearts were hurt
Laughing, picking, and acting like a jerk
No room for mercy only smirks.
Trapped in a mist of sin
There are no smiles now that your back is deign,
Only one name you truly can lean on and depend
Jesus will save your life again and again.
So the next time always say your prayers
There's only one who truly cares.
When night falls once again,
Your heart and mind
Won't be covered in sin.
Before you sleep make sure you pray
There is only one way
To keep the devil and his legion at bay,
Shout Jesus' Holy name,
That devil won't dare stay!
So don't be a fool
By allowing yourself to be used,
He doesn't need a reason

No certain time or season
Nothing you do will ever please him.
Jesus is faithful,
Why would you leave Him?

MIRACLES

The impossible can happen
If you believe in GOD,
When you began to pray
Repent for your sins
Let the Lord have his way
It's your heart he hears
Not the words you say.
He's there every second
Every minute of the day
No need to remind him
His memory doesn't fade.
Rich or poor
Jesus came to save,
Five thousand was fed
With two fish and five loaves of bread.
He walked on water,
Gave the blind sight,
This is not half
Of what he's done for the Israelites.
Miracles can happen before your sights
Just try real hard to do what's right.
Dreams are not fantasies,
They can take flight.
Miracles can be seen
To let go you must believe,
Don't let the devil trick you
He'll always deceive.
God will do all but fail
He gives you a choice: Heaven or Hell.
He was nailed to the cross for you and me
After three days he rose,
Now we're free.
The gate is open to eternity

Miracles are there, can't you see?
Jesus is here; He'll never leave!
Open your heart
So you can receive.

MOTHERLESS CHILD

If I were big enough, I would fight sickness
To the point of putting myself at a risk,
When I think back on my mother's last kiss.
Death took her away,
I miss her every single day.
Why couldn't life let her stay?
I just needed enough time to say,
Mommy dearest, I truly love you
And it's her words
Of encouragement that pulled me through.
Everything in life I would want to do.
I miss the smell of her hair,
I miss that fact that she really did care.
I miss the taste of her food,
I miss her voice that always soothe.
My mom drove away my blues,
We were an unbeatable team that could never lose.
She suffered so long and hard,
From the beginning until the end.
Every beautiful single part…
Who would have thought grave was so cold?
I remember touching her hand, hard as coal.
As pretty as the flowers although it took minutes.
"I felt like they were hours,"
Her spirit has been release to the highest power.
There's apart of me, will never be complete
It's the side of my heart that forever will weep.
Because my mom is every thump and beat.
You never realize, "how much a mother is missed
Until the day you become motherless!"

MY BABY'S BABY

The eyes of my baby's baby
Reveal a vision only I can see
The fact that he loves another and not me
He's always been unfaithful, but I can't let him be
I feel him throughout my body
My muscle cry out for him
He's so tall, tight nice and slim
My mother would always say
"How can you love a boy?"
That does nothing, but play
Then he likes to have things his own way
I can only remember that day
In the month of May
When we made love in a bale of hay
You set my heart on fire
Rolled my soul like a tire
The power he sent burn deep inside
It blinded me from seeing his lies
Now every time I look in his child's eyes
A piece of me slowly dies
I can't stay on this roller coaster ride
To father a baby then get up and leave
Take the mist of air you gave for him to breathe
Never ever supplying his needs
The back of your crack is all he's seen
He could never pick you out from the rest
Yet you say you know what's best
Then in the same breath, ask for a blood test
I'm truly sick and tried of your mess
Be a man and stand up strong
So your baby won't be raised alone
How long before you see you're wrong?
Don't wait too late to come home

Because if you do
My baby will grow up and throw stones
But I'll mold him into a man from the bone!

MY BEST FRIEND

Once in my life I had everything
The man of my life had gave me a ring.
We were happy and in love this was true.
My man and I were stuck together like glue.
There was not a happier two,
On my right sat my man,
On my left was my best friend.
Who would have guess I would be betrayed?
Who know the way my best friend would behave?
A man comes with risks.
Just like opening and closing your fist,
One blink and there's something you've missed.
Nothings for sure and never his kiss.
But my best friend was like my sister you see.
When you look at her,
You see apart of me,
I never knew she'll take my man and leave.
I saw all the signs but didn't read,
There was no way I could have believed.
Now I think what I could have had
How my best friend made my life so sad.
It hurts to bad to even get mad.
Love is blind when coming from both sides.
Especially, when you let your heart guide.
Don't want to question because of your pride
Every thought you fight to hide.
Although you know the truth deep in your mind.
A man will cheat, it don't matter if you're fine.
They have no respect for a woman's mind.
That fuzz ball between her legs,
This is what makes most men misbehave.
But my best friend should have put him in his place.
Not go to mush in his face,

All my secrets she could wait to taste.
She never saw me, only what was in his pants.
It didn't take long for me to understand.
Never again will we be friends,
Both of them have severed my hands.
I see her for the slut she is,
He's a boy and will never be a man.
So, I walk away with a lesson on life.
Choose your enemy once, your friend twice.
Watch what they say, never take advice,
"There's real love, but it comes with a price!"

MY DEATH IS LIFE

From the day I was born
Without my parents knowing
I was waiting to die,
Float on my wings in Heaven's Sky,
Fear and pain won't say goodbye
There is no sorrow or tears to cry,
Mom and Dad please just try.
Let me say a little about myself
I've inherited decomposing health.
See my transplant was good
The organ did all it could
My body rejected it,
I knew that it would.
I gave up on the will to live
My body is rotting
From the inside every inch I feel.
This is my bill of rights
Freedom comes without a fight
Internally, death has consumed me,
Hollow inside the human eye can't see
This desperate urge is my plea.
I must walk down this path holding my own
Firm mind on doing it all alone.
Inhaling death filling my lungs
My battle is over,
Yours has just begun.
A disease so hideous, it's marked by the beast
Patience has prepared me for the big feast.
In this world life's chained to grief
Every heart beat spells relief.
This is not a torment
But a laugh for peace!

MY PARENTS NAG

Everyday it never fails
My parents won't let me live
I feel so frail.
I can't think for myself
Unless I check in,
I feel locked down
I just can't win.
Every discussion is offensively blunt,
I'm just speaking my mind
This is not a stunt.
My parents look hard, trying to see,
But the part they miss
Is the heart of me?
Everything I say is under a scope
Why do grown-ups
Think all kids do dope?
If I ask to go somewhere
It always has to be ratified,
You look for a chaperone
Like I need an alibi.
Please notice I will tell you no lies
My life is open to you
I have nothing to hide.
My body raging fear
Won't give you a surprise,
It would be just like
Pouring lye in my own eyes.
What part of me you don't want free?
Please let me know,
I'll cut it off to leave
Oh, my dearest mom,
I just can't breathe.
I love both of you with all my might

But you shoved me in
This tiny small pipe
I don't want to argue and fight,
Just don't hold me so tight,
Believe in me,
I can do right!

NINA

My Dear Nina,
You were supposed
To be my protector,
My leader!
How could things have gotten out of hand?
It's not you I disapprove of,
It's where your heart stands.
The deepness of your wombs
There, your madness consumes
It's not me you want to hate
You just can't see clear
In your mental state.
Where did your love go?
Why don't your feelings flow?
In your eyes envy grows
What you've missed, you'll never know
To begin to heal
The real you must show.
I can't erase your past
Moments in time,
My pain will last.
I refused to hide behind your mask
A mind that's been so badly abused
Nailed down tortured and used.
Cold, chipped, cracked weight
Frightened with stony breaks
Invisible cracks
Of memories faced,
Let's not compete
This is not a race
Our blood's the same
I don't want your place.
Share with me this victory

Mold is a part of me
In your history
Our minds are different
When will you see?
Forgiving your pain
Sets me free,
Chain of greed
Has planted a seed,
Lost mixed soul
We're both in need!

NORMAL

Who really has the right to define normal?
What makes you think your normal is formal?
You're blinded by your denial
Open your mind and see the child
Take a moment to get to know
The very person you're calling slow
Ordinary and different have never been friends
Typical and common are on the same hand
A person I.Q.
Doesn't make them a women or man
How hard is it to understand,
Every one is average to some degree
That gives you no right to be little me
A learning disability is not a disease
It's another way of saying you have special needs
You can only feel inferior
If that's what you believe
No one can take anything from you
Unless you allow them to
The words disable
It don't spell out your unstable
So don't go through life putting them on a label
God created us all
And in every last one of us he found favor
So don't trace a disfigured face
Because you feel perfect at your pace
Jesus is the only one that can create
No man could ever take His place
Were all apart of the human race
So before you judge, trace your base
Jesus Grace has saved us all
No one's better or too small
We all have faults we can recall!

OLYMPICS

What is your deepest fear?
Riding yourself the entire year.
Reaching in to rob your soul,
Moment of truth no one can hold.
All you're hard work, like a statue.
That body you've molded,
Fear can taste you from head to toe.
Big deep breathes nice and slow.
Pushing yourself to the bitter end,
Its matters not the cost you must win.
The days are beginnings on angels wind.
If you fail, it will be four years
Before you can try again…
The competition is strong,
So many teens women and men;
Across the world stiff necks
Strong chins….
This history will never give,
What you waited for and beat to live.
Nerves of steel, time to kill
Emotion on life you truly feel.
The only essence is your durable will
All natural no drugs or pills,
"Just say no," is the real deal,
100% of health is your thrill.
Your all is on the line, time to let go.
Every second you must keep control.
Remember your reaching for the gold.
Failure and victory both want to dance.
Believe in your heart, only one can stand.
Put on your best,
Before you reach out you hand…
The four steps you need

Before you succeed,
All are connected in a family seed.
Motivation leans on determination,
Preparation feeds on destination.
The hold team is a part of you.
There is nothing you can't do,
Time is an essential only you can choose!

ON BENDED KNEES

Praying for a change as long as we can remember.
The victory is not clear; it's a blur
As the bloody sea of struggles are driven.
Every since the days of slavery,
We have been praying to God to change their ways.
Why do we separate people with aids?
Men and women we think are gay
Jesus died and arose for everyone may be saved.
Forever praying for freedom,
Not knowing the battle is already won
Can't ease the spirit of those that hung.
So we march for our no rights run,
We still have separated funeral homes.
This is another way of making blacks feel alone.
Even in death peace can not be found.
No unity, "Even when death has put us in the ground"
When will we feel each other?
Reach out to embrace our brothers…
The floor is worn with two deep holes,
Constantly passing down stones that's told.
To the one and only who controls,
Jesus the keeper of our soul.
In all this world blacks are suffering,
Yet people are blind to it,
They don't want it to be seen.
When will this state release their fear?
Admit their wrong free and clear.
Life itself is like a chain that connects,
You're never safe until you give respect.
For every living soul on God's green earth.
But the beginning is believe no man is first.
In doing this you'll see God's light….
"This will make you blind to *white is right!*"

ONE, TWO, THREE

I've been having sex
Since I was about fourteen.
No respect for number one, "which is me."
Although I wasn't on the pill,
I would still have sex at will.
I never thought I would get pregnant.
But I knew something was wrong.
Because I stayed sick.
"The fact of the matter,"
I don't know "who the father is!"
I'm not even close to a hint,
The first two I slept with were brothers.
They were never faithful to me.
Just true to each other,
Three, four, five, six, seven, eight and nine
They all ran a train on me,
At the same time.
I know I've slept with
Over thirty different men.
I wouldn't know where to start.
Or how to begin
All my life I've felt like a loser…
I could never get ahead and win.
I started so young, I just couldn't stop.
But now I wish I could turn back the clock.
You look for love in all the wrong places.
Searching hard in the different faces.
I'm only nineteen and I look thirty-two.
All the abuse "my body's been through."
Now, I have a child, what will I do.
I don't know who could be the father.
I've slept with so many men, why even bother.
From this point here on out.

I will be faithful to myself "without a doubt."
Being proud of who I am is what it's about.
I've learned a lesson, take another route.
I suffered to carry my baby,
Who better to owe but me.
So I must learn all over
How to be a lady!

ONLY A FEW LEFT

Through out history we were raised on the land.
We made our clothes and tinsels with our hands
The land, "is how our people survived."
A world away from everything even our own tribe.
But we were tricked with the white man's lies.
They stole our women and forced them to have sex.
When they were already promise,
To an Indian man with respect.
Our people are strong and free
But it was hard for them to see.
They just could not let us be,
We were hated before there were slaves.
They scalped our heads and made our women maids.
So many of my people buried in unmarked graves.
We used arrows and they used guns.
Its been very close but they still won
They took my people and locked them on reservations
We were prisoners of hearts of hate.
They purposely stole our will and fate.
America has never been our country,
We were forced to participate.
Our language that we spoke couldn't be understood.
So to put words in our mouth,
They surely would.
America wasn't the founder of this land.
The Indians we were first or what you call the red man.
It's only a handful of the first tribe,
And who will give account for all these lies.
This world seems to pacify,
They will answer for it.
Like weeds to grass and trees to sticks.
"Evil opens that door,"
"When you do wrong,"
It comes three scores more!

ORDINARY DIFFERENT

You are unusual and unique,
What you sow you'll reap.
It's nice you practice what you preach
The way you bond with others,
Is like a child that bond with their mother.
Closer then sisters and brothers.
Your giving is something else,
You're giving apart of you
Until there's nothing left.
Always opening your mind
To think how others felt
To see someone in pain,
It makes your eyes weep.
Pushing to reach that higher step.
You sacrifice, "everything you have to help."
Real life hasn't mold people of your kind,
Deep and far in a distance,
Rolled away from time.
You're like an artist that does wood carving.
Taking the food out your mouth,
To keep someone else from starving.
You have no boundaries,
Depriving yourself to supply others in need.
You've yield to be a true friend,
Know until the very end.
Forever beside you I will stand.
A rare ruby indeed,
That's ordinary different,
"You and only you hold the heart in me!"

OUR FAMILY

Behind these walls
Held in captivity
Is the real side of our family?
Though hidden never to be seen
The search for fulfillment our hearts
Deeply fling.
Covered in exclusion
Scrubbing to be clean,
Exception without conclusion
Justified no means.
My kids are the strength
That holds our house together,
Morning, noon, night
Don't matter the weather.
I've built a habit
I'm not proud of
Internally it deprives me of love.
Because of my soft heart you see
It takes away the peace in free.
Wounds open
I fight to protect,
When I speak my mind
Our family thinks it is disrespect.
I feel like my kids and me
Are seen as rejects,
Everything they do is not perfect
We all make mistakes
What do they expect?
This decision is not theirs to make.
The closest sister I've ever known
Has build, herself a wall of stones
Childlike, yet she's grown
When she realizes the truth

She'll be all alone.
Then our family will still be
Because our lives depends on Jesus,
Who died to set us free!

PRAYING HANDS

There is so much power in these hands.
They can destroy devils and demons.
Even bring down the strongest man.
There is nothing that's a match
Once these two hands, "have been dispatched."
Jesus gave me this gift,
And when I put them together
All my burdens have been lifted
Nothing is more faithful and true
My God always knows what to do.
Trust in him and He will see you through,
Because his anointing breaks the yolk,
Believe me, my brother, there is always hope.
He may not come when you want him,
But He's always on time
These are facts not made up lines.
This is the truth; Jesus can do all but lie.
So wipe those tears from your eyes,
Mr. Bills says, "I'm due today,"
You call up Loan and he says there no way
Put your hands together and begin to pray.
Watch Jesus take over and Mr. Bills get his paid.
The prostitute turning tricks on the streets,
Only because she needs food to eat.
Bring together your two hands
Let Jesus, "give you the victory dance."
No need to sell yourself to man,
Jesus will always understand.
He took two fish and five loaves of bread.
Fed over five thousand,
Believe in your heart that he's not dead…
A mountain of food will fall upon you head.
He's on call twenty-four seven,

Put those hands together
And pray to Him in Heaven.
So don't you ever worry
About anything not even food,
"He is King of Kings and believe He rules!"

REAL FRIEND

Were you ever really there?
Did you really ever care?
All I had to give I would share
The secrets you've told.
I'll forever deeply hold
With a friend like you
Who needs an enemy?
Every since I met you
You've been my rivalry
Leading me in the wrong direction.
Only in it for your protection.
You act like you knew everything,
It's only your projection.
You've put me at a crossroad,
Thinking if I should leave you in the cold.
My gentle heart you stole,
I was there to console
A comforter to the body and soul.
In spite of your mental blows.
I thought of you as family,
But closer than my blood line.
You tricked me in front of my eyes
Abused trust…
You hit me from my blind side,
Now you see this world,
Don't revolve around you.
More to life, then what you want to do.
A real friend wouldn't make you choose.
There would be no competition,
So no one would loose.
There's so much damage and harm you've caused.
Internal greed is what it's called,
There's nothing beneath you when you fall.

For your feelings of no sympathy,
I've invented a remedy.
Mixed with merciful reality…
That you're no good for me
The conclusion of this lesson
Has really been a blessing?
There are boundaries
You shouldn't cross
And a real friend wouldn't test them out!

REFLECTION

When I look at myself
I see what I want to be
A thin person that looks very good
Watches what she eats
The way she should
Superstitious this is not I
There's no way to explain
Or began to say why
I love to eat all the time
I've been this way since I was about nine
Now that I'm in my prime
People stare at me like I'm a sign
I'm addictive to food
I just can't stop
Even if I tried, my body will go into shock
Because of my emptiness
I take internal risk
My addiction to food has stolen my health
All this fat around my organs
I can only blame myself
I eat until my belly swells
And I look like a two-ton whale
I eat until I can hardly stand
The fluid from my body swells my hands
My gluttonies has stole
Every drop of happiness
You never realize you're alone
Until you think about what you've missed?
There are times I eat until I vomit
And feel really sick
Then when I can't get enough food
My body goes into fits
Mr. Obesity is an eating disorder that always tease

Only because he knows food makes me pleased
My mouth stays on fire,
Torturing aches, so much my tongue burns.
As my stomach starts to churn
In my mind I'm deeply hurting
Twisted and disfigured is my self-esteem
Because all my life I've been treated so mean
The people who mistreat me are foul
I have to love myself
By creating my own style
There are no superior beings
Everyone is not going to be lean
So no one has the right
To make me feel unclean
We all have a part of us
Were not proud of
And because no ones perfect
We should love, love, love!

SATIN SHEETS

You've tricked a weak minded man,
With your suggestion.
And invisible hands in his pants.
Coming out like you wanted to help.
When all the time you knew how your heart felt.
"Baiting him into your room,"
"To roll in your bed of doom,"
"Candle lights all around,"
You knew what was about to go down.
"Giving off your mating sound"
Full of every *disease* in the book.
"But he's blinded by your looks"
You don't have a heart, and you're a crook.
Red light special on Monday through Saturday.
Whips, handcuff, oil, chains and lingerie
"Queen of all the whores,"
The fact is you made weak men slaves.
When the lights go out at dawn on Sunday.
You're getting ready for church,
Putting on your nice long suit.
To cover up your dirt,
Even shout and stand up to testify.
When the preacher preach you start to cry.
Your only fooling yourself sin can't hide.
When you open your mouth,
"Those demons fly out and high,"
Real Saints know your watering your lies.
Satin sheets tends to hold dirt,
"No matter what!"
You can clean it, but nothing will ever work.
In the end look in the mirror,
"Who do you really hurt!"

SET YOUR GOALS

Never set limits on what you can do,
It deprives the beauty that lives within you
Set Your Goals!
Everyone has an inner strength
To believe in yourself
There is no length
Set Your Goals!
Dreams are reality
That wait in the wind
Every morning you wake
Life starts again
Set Your Goals!
Nothing is impossible
Just be yourself
Know in the end
Success is all that's left
Set Your Goals!
Struggles fight you on every hand
Remember there's no limit,
Your best will stand
Set Your Goals!
Always stay true
Nothing can stop you
Every thought in your head
Everything you do
Set Your Goals!
Achieve is a word
You should never lose
The rule to choices
Take your time and choose
Set Your Goals!

SILENT KILLER

Have you met the robbers of life?
They sneak up on you
Like thieves in the night
And hits you hard from you blind sight
Cigarettes, Cocaine, alcohol are their names
They run together so tight
You can call them a gang
Mr. Party never shows up unless they're there
As if Mrs. Different Homes could really care
Cancer is as patient as splitting hairs
It's only a matter of time
Before your whole body you'll share
Let me break down the good old boys for you
Because so many people don't have a clue
There's no force you can choose
Mr. Addiction has no right to rule
Cigarettes laced with Ms. Nicotine
Whose selfish and cruel dipped in mean?
When they're together Black Tar is the star
They will eat and stick to your lungs by far
Holding Mr. Smoke in your body like a jar
Cocaine the queen of seduce
She really gives men and women a boost
Relaxes them making their body loose
Miss Cocaine love to make your nose bleed
All your internally organs she'll feed
Your crave won't go away
Because she's planted her seed
Her secret is she's eating your brain
And pretty soon you won't remember anything
Seeing things that's not even there
Nothing is grounded even you float in the air
A lemon head that taste like a lime

Miss Cocaine will have you
Selling you body for a dime
You really should stop and read the sign
Because you'll be introduced to Mr. Crack this time
Mr. Alcohol is really the tease
Man or woman he brings you to your knees
Flavors beyond your wildest dreams
Yet his real face can't be seen
He tricks a lot of people, they think he's clean
He's the lover of livers
And will make your body free
Once your liver is nice and hard
Everything is drunk even your heart
Then the real battle will start
There's nothing to filter your blood
I truly hope you've said goodbye,
To everyone you love
Pick out a coffin and flowers
Because it's only a matter of hours
Before you float up that tower
Then rain down with the morning showers
There grave has the power
Alcohol, Cocaine, Cigarettes
Is nothing but extra bags
If you're a friend of theirs, that's so sad
Because they don't care about your health
When their finish with you
There will be nothing left
Always remember
To look out and take care of self
You owe you if no one else
Just Say No has offices all around,
Take the notion and visit them in town!

SIXTEEN

There once was a little girl
Who lived with her mother
Her father had left
And she didn't have any brothers.
The little girl's mother had a man friend.
Who moved in with them to give her a hand.
Her mother got attached to him,
And would put everything out on a limb.
He meant the world to her,
Even more then her little girl.
One day she left for work,
And this man began to flirt.
He caused that child a deep ridden hurt.
Grave spit in your face
You're a disgrace to the mother race.
Leaving your child with a stranger.
Less then a man… human waste.
You force your child into a life at fast pace.
The little girl left home at only sixteen.
Real short, nice and lean,
This run away had nowhere to stay.
Tired and hungry and needing somewhere to lay.
That's when pimps came to say.
If you give a little play,
I know how to help you in many ways.
Not knowing what she was going to do.
She did not know what she had to go through.
But she felt she could not loose.
At least she would have food,
Selling her body and doing drugs,
This child emotions were worn like a rug.
"Self-esteem none to speak of!"
She had already been deprived of love.

A young life robbed to be old
Hollow on the inside they stole her soul
Nothing but emptiness to hold.
So much to live for
Knowledge she never learned or explored.
Now her changes has went out the door.
You carried this baby for nine months.
Yet you're the first one to give her up.
What mother wouldn't care
That's your child her reflection you share
This cross of sin your child will bear.
Is on your head every single hair!

SPLIT SECOND LOST

In a fraction of a minute your life could change.
Emerging from your heart with a deep ridden pain.
Facing day by day reflection of shame,
Encouraging words that make you lame.
What now can you possibly hope to gain?
A view, "of your backside in a frame."
Crippled from head to toe.
Every inch of you has let go,
Who can say and who truly knows?
"Reality can run fast or slow."
Moving quickly as the wind blows.
No point of how it will flow.
This new prison is colder than snow.
Beside friends, yet alone,
You're own waste feels like home.
Rigid edge, ash foam bones
Hiding behind your teeth of chrome
Empty my bladder, clean my mess
Fluff my pillows so I can rest,
"I can't feed myself,"
"I always need help,"
It's like I'm a child going through the first steps
A machine pumps my lungs with air
No scratch can stop my itchy hair,
Nothing to do but lay there and stare.
Time has spit, "death in the air,"
I can't help but think of it without a care.
Am I really alive, how much can I bare?
I fuss and scream constantly,
Begging for attention is my plea
My throat dries out, my mucus freezes
My lips are chapped and need to be greased.
I know it's hard to imagine, if you're not going through.

Folding your arms saying,
What can I do?
Just like this accident happened to me,
What if it happens to you?
Don't frown like dried up bacon,
Face of questions, like a wrinkle raisin...
Get off the pointy fingers and give donations....
The real part of life sits "nervous and pacing."
You never know what split second is waiting!

STRESS

Nerves raised like straight course hair,
Muscles aches from the looks and stares
Every word is without a thought or care,
You're feeling so naked boneless and bare,
Some many places to go, but lost on where
Here, STRESS is clear!
Your husband misses work to go and play
Your lunch looks like the vomit from yesterday
You've used orange paint instead of hair spray
Your nails popped off with crazy glue
Because your boss was working you like a mule
Here, STRESS is clear!
You know you're fifty pounds over weight,
Yet you couldn't help, but eat a whole pound cake
Then had the nerve to lick the plate
Your friends trying to find you another mate.
So they set you up on a blind date
Turns out he's drowned several women in a lake
Here, STRESS is clear!
FBI most wanted did an interview on him
On the street he's known as tiny Tim
One peanut and a half of slim Jim
Here, STRESS is clear!
You took a overdose on your Hormone pills
Now you yell and scream,
Because of uncontrollable thrills,
Working over time to keep it real,
At night searching for five finger deals.
Here, STRESS is clear!
Mask your face with mud that turn to clay
Missed your deodorant for a can of raid
Now it will be months before you can shave
Every morning face with Mr. Stress

Riding you like a donkey,
Never giving you peace can't get any rest
Your whole life seems like it's in a mess
Honey, it's a hallucination
Twisting your mind
If it persist for seven days get help it's time!
Here, STRESS is clear!

THE BATTLEFIELD

We are going here to fight for our country.
This is our right to keep us free
So many are blind and refused to see.
The only thing standing between captivity,
Is the urge to will that lives in us
To defend our rights for freedom we must.
We step out knowing,
Every moment could be our last.
You have to keep your mind focus,
Because you know you have a great task.
Revolutions have always resembled the past.
The enemies always hide behind a mask.
Weapons of victory in our hands,
Bundles of courage so we will stand.
Cowards of fear can run far from here.
We have a purpose and it's crystal clear.
Accepting a war is beyond our control,
But true to our flag we shall hold.
Conflicting combat is our habit,
"Our mind of skills unfold like magic!"
The welfare of the United States.
Must take a front seat even if it seals our fate.
We were bred and trained by the best,
We stay prepared and passed the entire test.
We are a fighting machine that needs no rest.
There is no way we will take anybody's mess,
When you come to do battle with us,
We shall beat your best.
"Because we give it our all and nothing less!"

THE FIGHT

When my struggles and burdens
Were too hard to bare
I felt life left behind me with despair,
Jesus showed me He was there.
He swooped me up in his arms
He sings to me his favorite songs
This sinful world
Can't do me any harm
Around my neck
His cross of Angel's charm
When I'm in danger
His Holy Spirit alarms.
No matter what evil
I walk upon,
They yield to Jesus
Because He's the one.
He rose after three days
Of being crucified and hung,
This war on earth has just begun,
But children of God
The battle has been won.
Don't take the mark of the beast
On your hand or head,
Though he may temp you
With water and bread.
The spirit doesn't need food
The flesh is weak
Cries to be fed
Close your mind and shield your heart,
You're being mislead
Listen to what the Holy Spirit said.
See the anti-Christ for what he is
Your precious soul he's out to steal

Satan's heart has been revealed.
Trick of love, Hate of steel
Forever torture, this you will feel.
Jesus' love, He freely gives,
Bow on your knees repent to live.
Satan's people are the walking dead
For eternity you'll burn
In Hell's fire bed!

THE LOVE OF MY LIFE

A man stopped me today to say,
When will you give your heart away?
Is there a price he must pay?
What must he lay down to get your play?
You hold these secrets in a shell,
I'll take a bath in the lake of hell.
My precious emeralds,
I would gladly sell....
I'll eat a million lizard's tails,
I'll suck the slime out of snails.
You say you're taken,
Why won't you tell.
Are you afraid?
This love of yours would fail...
"Or your relationship is much too frail!"

I took a moment to clear my head,
I thought about what he had said
Knowing all his words were lies
I didn't want to make him cry.
I looked in his eyes, then gave a sigh
What makes my love so untouchable you see?
He's greater than you and I could ever be
Besides knowing my faults,
He supplies my needs.
Without asking, he knows I'm pleased
Always on call 24hours a day.
He never leaves my side,
Especially when I pray.
Anytime I need my love
He's always there.
It's when I'm in trouble,
He picks me up with care.

All my pain, "He bares and shares,"
This I know no man would dare.
Every tear that falls from my eyes,
He wipes it with his Heaven's Skies.
Because on him the joy of happiness
In life realize…
To accept him is a priceless prize.
You're never alone,
When he's on your side.

The man looks at me wanting to understand.
I began to shout out loud and dance,
I could see his smile
Start to expand.
Then I told my secret, to this man.
He's God over all this grand land.
I remember the first day I took his hand.
The only true love of my body and soul
True devotion I deeply hold.
Nothing in my life has been the same,
Every moment of the day…
I sing his name!
"JESUS, JESUS, JESUS"

THE MARCH

My ancestors two feet
Walk in a straight line
To change the schools for all times
They were beat because they wanted
A fair education.
We believe if we stood together
We could change them
At the risk of being hung by a limb
Day by day our future grew dim
Being spit on and kicked to the side
We held our heads up high with pride
In our eyes freedom was on our side
We let our will power be our guide
Some of us were sprayed with water hoses
The racism really took toil
But we never gave in or let go
A lot of us were locked in jail
In our history we do tell
So don't drop out or give in when you fail
School is important,
Many people paved the way
So you can learn and have a right to stay
Times are different from back then,
So many things have came to an end
If you don't give in you'll surely win
The past is not meant to cripple
It can never make you slow
Time can only push you further
And teach you how to grow
Knowledge is information
That should always flow
Or regardless of your color
You'll be left in the cold,

Always time will continue to roll.
So remember education
Should be your number one goal!

THE MISTRESS

All of my struggling life
I have truly loved my wife,
But stolen one night
The pure beauty before my sight
I've lost my will to do what's right
Trapped in a caged fight.
Although I go home everyday
My mind and body just won't stay
The mistress is rooted deep within me
I can't let her go I can't let her be.
The stars in heaven twinkle up above
Every time we're together and make love,
I crave to feel her kisses and hugs.
She's like a honey tree
I'm drawn to her like a bee
A part of my soul runs free
The look in her eyes drives nails in me.
My hunger for love will never leave
She's my root and I'm her seed
No way will my wife understand or believe
The vision before her she never sees.
My mistress' poison reigns
To live without her drives my pain.
I've broken up our happy home
Now my kids may be raised alone.
There is no controlling these hands
They define the fact I'm a man.
But the reality remains
I work hard and try to be true,
But being a man comes with rules
Both of my heads make their own moves.
A man loses strength with every women he lays
Then when she wants him

His parts are forced to pay,
This is how it is when you play.
Mr. Disease visits several times a year,
Condoms run from me with fear
Playing with what I truly hold dear,
My emptiness that can never be filled.
Why does my family have to see my shame?
What could I have ever hoped to gain?
A mistress is like maggots
Eating until you're hollow on the inside
Looking like less than a man
No strength left or pride
Dripping in blacken lies,
Weeping eyes of a man that cries
Once he faces life and realize
That mistress he let ride
Is really a lust demon in disguise!

THE MOON

The only beauty that touches the sun,
Consumed, rejuvenating energy,
Gravitation flows back the light that's shunned.
For centuries scientists have been stunned,
The fascination far and beyond,
Their understanding have just begun.
Consistent and unpredictable in all aspects.
But in the midst of darkness,
It reflects…
Some say the moon affect peoples' signs.
Maybe even changes their minds,
It goes further, then the beginning of time.
Acute, uncontrollable in every way,
It changes when it chooses.
Sometimes everyday…
Connecting to the sky, hanging so free.
No one knows how, "Only the Almighty,"
Stars dance with the moon,
And all around.
A mystical silence not known by sound!

THE OCEAN

Have you ever really
Looked at the ocean?
The waves moving
All different motions
Silky smooth,
Like oil mixed with lotion
Shivering cold, get the notion?
The sound of the waves,
A natural love potion.
The ocean I feel
Is hard to understand
What besides gravitation
Keeps it off land.
Something this beautiful,
Could never be created
By a man's hands.
The wave moves like a dance
The breeze blows from it
Feels like Heaven's fan.
An entire separate world,
Out in the sea
A different creation
From you and me
An environment where mother nature
Takes the responsibility
Unlike what takes place,
In our society.
So strong, intuitive, powerful and free
So wholesome, natural, fresh and clean
Filled with plants, mammals,
And varieties of breeds;
Always something new
Another origin or species.

The ocean to me
Is like a part of the wild,
Uncommon and distinct
With its own style!

THE OTHER WOMAN

Everyday my husband comes in,
He's tired from beginning to end.
We don't make love like before
I'm in the bed,
And he takes the couch or floor.
What am I doing wrong,
Why does he leave me alone.
I've done everything I can to improve.
Yet his heart can't be soothe.
We've only been married a few months.
I can't walk out and give up.
What could have turned his love to hate?
He never was like this when we used to date.
This man I see, I really don't know
So many different personas in a row.
A shameful relationship covers us,
There's something he wants to say,
Every question we start to fuss.
After all he was my first,
In his eyes a foreign lust.
This particular day I was sitting outside.
Gallons of tears drowns my eyes.
Then I see my man's ride,
There was someone sitting close and beside.
I got in my car and follow him down the road.
What do you know whoa and behold?
I see why now he's been treating me so cold.
In his arms another man he holds.
Now, "the reason is so clear"
That inner voice, I never did hear
This is why I couldn't get any play.
Because my husband really is gay.
Although he could never say,

I know I saw it in all his ways.
Even on that first day…
So many men have another side,
One he shows and the other he hides.
So women open your eyes really wide
Pay close attention to soft-spoken lines.
You'll see it's only a matter of time,
Before that man shed his skin,
And the other woman stands behind.
"If you blink you'll miss the sign!"

THE RING

As I put on my gloves
I've removed from my heart any type of love.
We hit our hands together in the ring,
Then begin to stare at each other real mean.
Listening to the referee say lets keep it clean.
Two men beating their brains,
So one over the other prove their name.
What can they possibly hope to gain?
Someone's freak show,
Knocking each other to the floor,
So much damage, what's the real score.
The fact you could go blind
A second slower than time.
Money is the root of everything
For the right price
Two monkeys will swing.
That green keeps our greed alive,
This is how our American people survive.
What happened to hope and a ounce of pride?
Every single tear pain cries,
A ring of heroes changing places.
Each tick slowly puts something new in place.
One BIG, hungry rat race,
Sweating and shaking turned by fate.
Tempted to entice, rolled to rejuvenate
Holding your thoughts right,
What's the real price?
Reality shows out bid for life!

THE STORM

Everywhere I turn
I seem to get badly burned
I try so hard
But I get attacked on every part
Here I search for an end,
Blinded in the dark
I know this point is just a start.
Ate up with infection
No guide for my protection
Out there is a cure
If I stay focused, I can steer.
Jesus didn't give me
A spirit of fear
I'm so trapped,
Pinned to the wall
I can't even remember peace,
Happiness never called
If ever I needed relief
My burdens are heavy
Covered in grief
Mixed up with a silent desire
In my heart, pain explodes with fire
I won't let go
There is a power much higher
Being a failure to thrive
Its force drives me to survive
No regrets of tears I've cried
There's nowhere to run,
No place to hide.
This hurricane that wants to seize
Hugs my life and brings me to my knees.
Through my faith,
This storm can't succeed

I'll hang on tight,
Until I'm freed!

THE WRITING ON THE WALL

Your skin may be dark
But you are blessed
Our people have the beauty mark
Your smooth black skin
Shines brighter than that midnight star.
Our struggles long, but we've come so far.
Don't let miss guided whites,
Tell you who you are.
White men can't understand you,
He don't even acknowledge,
The pain he put our people through.
Some of you seem to forget,
Just what the word freedom means.
Open your mind let me come clean.
The right to look
In the eye of white women.
Without being thrown in jail,
Then hear from the judge
Your black soul will rot in hell...
To have white men pass by you
And your body won't flinch.
If he says something wrong,
Speak up and don't clinch.
See, our ancestors went through a test.
So our generation won't suffer
The same mess.
Time has moved on, but slavery's not gone.
Engraved in our bone our slave song.
The clan is still here, leading the chiefs
But instead of sheets,
Different uniforms just like the police.
Take a moment...
What did they deliberately omit,

Have you ever seen a black president?
If a brother runs from the flag, he'll be lynched.
That red, white and blue,
Don't stand for you.
All these years playing you for a fool.
No matter what they say, or what they do
There is a side, you must choose.
This society we live in,
It has a system.
Do you know what that means?
Another word for get them!

TOO YOUNG

I'm too young to take care of a family.
When my dad walked out on my mom,
He walked out on me.
My mom has so many bills,
She's trying to work two jobs, which have made her ill.
But I love her for trying.
I refuse to stand by,
And watch my family while their dying.
Dad doesn't pay his child support.
He uses the system daily to extort.
I have to get a job,
Or "I'll end up going out there to rob."
My family lives in my heart,
There is no way; "I'm going to let them starve"
Welfare system loves to blame,
My mother for her shame,
When in reality,
They're the ones causing all the pain.
Saying, she shouldn't have had all those kids.
Why don't they stuff their mouth or use a lid?
I wouldn't have to work and go to school.
If they would give a little help and some food.
I still don't make enough, "to buy my mother's medicine."
It's only certain things, "that makes the systems bend,"
And I don't see Medicare with money to lend.
All we hear is our hands are tied.
Were doing all we can
"There's a process we must go by,"
Believe me, it's not a lie.
"It's not as easy as screwing in a bulb."
But here I stand, on the corner to sale drugs.
I do it because of the family, which I love
I'm too young to get a decent paying job.

221

So this looks better to me by far.
So before the government yells, lock them up
He needs to look closely at every bump.
In his system there he'll see the lumps.
I'm not saying selling drugs are good.
But I'm saying the system,
Needs to do what they should.
And then allow a brother to get out the hood!

TRAGEDY

Our birth of rage
Has survived into this day.
Pass the point of living through slaves.
We are putting ourselves,
In shallow graves.
The way this generation behaves,
Young people running from themselves.
Passing the blame on everything else.
Stealing the life the joy of being,
Trapped somewhere between,
Hidden cowardly can't be seen.
Shielding is the mask of driven mean.
Who can stop the killing of you?
Hold-ups and drive-bys too,
Time is short you need to choose.
You're the only one that can make you lose.
Malicious and cruel handicaps your heart.
Restrain with interest detaches your parts.
Raped by violence
The fact that people always resent,
Not knowing intelligence pays your rent.
Suddenly burst of understanding,
Forgets reality is for us to be free.
You're killing each other
Faster then growing weeds.
Snuffing out the living breath
Where death can be seen.
You can change your mind.
As fast as the wind blows
A split second of peace,
Your know the real test
"Is learning to let go!"

TRAPPED

I've been tied in this relationship
Always my husband, "says no lip!"
Do what I say—no questions ask?
I don't even know how our marriage has last.
He beats me all the time,
That should have been the first red sign.
Or when He gave me syphilis,
Even my mouth was full of pus.
I was sick for so many days,
But I had to get up and cook anyway.
Clean his house real good,
Run his bath water half way full.
I had so many treatments and different disease.
Still I haven't the strength to leave.
"He has lowered my self-esteem!"
I feel filthy, dashed with a lot of unclean,
Because I have no working skills
He thinks he can do what he feels.
My psychological needs are like a spill.
Who cares what's going on, it's about his will.
I crave for warmth and some type of love.
All he says, "is there's none to speak of!"
What if I get HIV, will he then cry for me?
I don't believe that even then he'll see.
I'm too old to turn back the clock.
It went on so long, how can I say stop
I'm on the edge ready to pop,
Here, "he knocks on kill me door"
Bloody revenge wrote all over the floor.
What sanity will even the score
"This man that I truly adore,"
But I just can't take it anymore.
I feel like a failure with no reason to live.

Every part of me to this man I did give.
We went together like head and brain.
Every part of my body reflect his name.
Covered in bed sores burnt on pain.
Drops of feces fall like rain,
I must unlock this gate of obsession.
Because in my imaginative world,
I'm driven into a deep depression.
I hope someone else, "learns from this lesson!"

TREASURED MOMENTS

Looking back on the days of my past.
Every single moment I wish could last.
You taught me manners,
And the way I should behave.
You never focus on the mistakes I made,
From the time I went from crawling to walking.
From babbling to talking,
"You never lost sight!"
Grandmothers like you
Always did what was right.
Even singing me to sleep at night.
Teaching me to do war with my mind.
Not with my hands
Use my intelligence to take a stand.
A man is not defined by what he shows.
But by the wisdom and knowledge he feeds to grow.
I went to school on the narrow,
And being straight.
Because, Grandmother, it's you I appreciate.
I could never cause you any disrespect,
You've always covered me in your cherished love net.
A person's characteristics are defined by their conduct.
But yours have taught me never to give up.
You're a priceless precious prize,
The day my mother gave me away
And I looked into your eyes,
We changed each other lives.
Here we're joined until the day one of us dies.
Just as beautiful as heaven skies,
More peaceful then the ocean shores.
Truly, Granny, it's you "I'll always adore."
Valued, honored, admired forevermore!

TWO-SIDED HEART

We are twins living in the same body
One of flesh and the other spirit you see.
Mr. Flesh loves to drink and get high,
Shooting needles in his arm
Every word from his mouth—a lie.
Sleeping with a different women everyday.
Treating his wife like "his maid"
Making his kids work like slaves,
His heart is headed for an early grave.
Mr. Flesh knows the word,
But acts like he never heard.
Damage deeper then his injury,
Because of his sin he'll never be free.
Yet "he tries to justify to me."
Mr. Spirit, which is I, I'm sold on Christ
Jesus excepted me long ago,
And now the word is my life.
I know without Him I have no life.
No sexual desire do I have?
When I'm around Flesh filth,
I sprint for a bath.
Flesh fights with me every day and in every way.
But because of my Spirit holiness,
Flesh can't stay.
They are both apart of the same being.
One nice and understanding,
The other hateful and mean.
Looking at each other and yet can't be seen.
So full of love, yet full of hate.
One's at peace, the other is on a verge,
Of a mental break.
Mr. Flesh holds death and grave will collect.
Mr. Spirit holds life and grave must show respect!

UNCLE TOM

Look in the mirror at you
You're not tired of playing the fool
The way you do your own people
Is down right rude
Denying your color won't make you free
Don't you know that's the first thing they see?
And they're shocked at what you're pretending to be
Killing you trying to please
While bringing our own people to their knees
They use one of our kinds to beat us down
When we look at you, we can't help but frown
You might as well paint your face white
Because you've already lost the fight
Trapped in the fact you don't want a change
Why would you not
Want to get rid of your slave name
Freedom ringed long ago
You're a minute behind and much to slow
When will you let go?
Every time they sound that dinner bell
Bossing your people with screams and yells
Pushing for them to work hard and fast
So your head position will continue to last
You're still their boy
How can you forget your past?
Wanting to stay a in-house slave
You don't want nothing more then to be their maid
Sometimes we remember
On the things that were wrong
Then we join hands singing
Our we shall over come song
We are still fighting for simple rights
All these years it's still not in our sight

To see our own kind,
Who don't want freedom to reign?
Hurts deeper then you'll ever know,
You have forgot our peoples stabbing pain
My dear brother,
As much as we have grain
Things are still basically the same
But instead of a rope to hang
It's the system their using to slain!

UNHEARD CRY

Several years ago, when my divorce was final
I had to assume a father role...
His dad was out of my life,
And there I was, "trying to raise him right."
I never knew about the other side of my son.
"Before I knew it," the war had begun...
My own child would beat me you see
And I better not try to stop him from leaving.
Or he would leave, me on the floor bleeding.
I am his own mother, He was my child from my womb."
Would he be the one to put me in my tomb?
I wanted to teach him respect,
But all my love, "he would always reject."
The child I carried for nine months,
Gave birth to and cleaned his rump.
Now has turned into a nightmare,
Even before his father left, I've always been there.
Every inch of me I would share,
Because he is my child and I really care.
The system protects the child,
It doesn't matter that they're out of control and wild
When you defend their wrong,
They feel, "this behavior is allowed."
So they stand up proud,
Parents' lives need to be saved.
So when they are raising a child
The system, "shouldn't make waves."
Because in the end
It's the child, "you put in the grave."
The bible says, "Honor thy Mother and Father,"
Or they will shorten their own days.
So it takes all of us
To teach our children to change their ways!

UNSEEN HANDS

Blinded to the human eye
The hand that can't be seen
Is the fact of the matter?
There's someone you can lean on
When you feel like all hope is gone
Your bills are due
There's no one to look to
You're so full of stress
And don't know what you're going to do
Little do you realize
There's someone higher that hears your cries!
In minutes your problem seems to dissolve
Everything in your life starts to revolve
Still you don't understand He's your true friend
And because of this you don't see His hand
You're struck down sick
With a contagious disease
It's paralyzed your body and your mind frozen
To sick to kneel on your knees
Can't focus so you can't read
All the doctors expect you to die
You've realize this and said goodbye
Only but one to make man into a lie
He just blows on your flesh
Your spirit floats high
You're healed from head to toe
And no one understands why
That hand that is invisible to man
The keeper of our soul
Only he controls
The whole world over looks
Because they just don't know
The spiritual eye can reveal
You must accept him

Of your own free will
He is the lifeline
That allows you to live
Until you repent you'll never feel
And you'll never see
That unseen hand is real!

VICTORY

I have the victory after two years
I accomplished all my hidden fears.
I used to drink like a fish,
But now that alcohol I don't miss.
I sold everything in my home,
I tried to fight this battle monster alone,
It's all I've ever been shown,
I grew up being abused,
Shot in the head remembering the blues.
Raised to believe I'll always lose
My heart was deeply bruised,
Because I know my bodies been used.
I never had pity for myself,
An empty bottle robbed of health.
I wanted to fit, "in that bottle of pain to hide."
It got additive and I lost my pride
Why would I ever have chosen this side?
It's a shame when you embalm your body.
"As a pass time or a hobby,"
"I nearly died because of this,"
"My liver lives on the black list,"
Death gave me a kiss that day,
cirrhosis of the liver moved out.
"He didn't want to stay"
Grace said, "I've been saved"
One tiny hair above my grave.
Memories told me
Good thing I changed my ways.
So, if you have any type of addictions.
It's important for you to listen.
Pay very close attention,
You don't have to be an addict
Get some help.
And take up a healthy habit!

VIP

Do you really know the difference?
Between a wife and a maid
Majority of men treat women like slaves
Counting down the night and days
Don't want to hear your lip,
And don't make any waves
All because of the bills he pays
When he enters the house from the jump
You know better than to be sitting on your rump
His food needs to be hot on his plate
It better already be ready, he don't like to wait
Dessert is a must; it has to be already baked
If you fail in any of these tasks,
You've made a mistake
When he's ready, he expects his bath water warm
Warming his bed and setting his alarm
He don't care how you feel
If it's not done, he means you harm
He feels he don't owe you anything
Your never hear a thank you
Small minded as he is,
He wants to do what he choose
In his book of rights, there are no rules
Only you have don't and he has all the do's
Your never ever hear him say please
If you don't like it, then leave
He wants you to beg and crawl on your knees
Scrubbing floors with your hands,
Your housework is never enough.
Cause he is the man,
Treating you like a child that don't understand
Yet he claims he's your biggest fan
Ladies, if you feel this is your house

Set him straight, cause you're his spouse
Your can of patience just ran out
A marriage is not a play
Be careful what you do and what you say
Love is something that can die or grow
A little respect can plug up all the holes
Good women don't stand in a row
So watch yourself before you let her go!

VOICES WITHIN

What are you telling me to do?
Why would you want me to hurt you?
If I kill you, I'll die too
We are not different were one in the same?
So we both will lose,
All of you are against me
I must bleed myself free
Pushing me over the edge
Playing tricks in my head
Trying to make me look mad
Don't fluff my coffin pillow
I'm not dead,
If you cut your wrist
I'll give you a kiss
If you hang from this rope
I'll help you float
One thing for sure
You definitely won't choke
You're our host; we're not going anywhere
This is our body too, so you have to share
All the abuse I suffered as a child
No protection, it was condoned and allowed
My fears and pains turned to personalities
And every last one of them lives in me
Because I didn't get therapy
It has grown like a wild weed
Until every inch of my brain has been seized
I can't rationalize on what's wrong and right
Inside my body a raging fight
Courage won't swing by and defend
My whole life dangles in the wind
You know when you're facing the end
There is no way they will cease

I'm trying to pull my will, but I can't reach
Who give the lessons, which they teach?
My voices of insane as they preach
No one deals with how I feel,
The voices in my head are real
In order to help me, my heart they must heal
The doctors just want to give me a crazy pill
One that's for sure, it will make me ill
Why let my fate be sealed?
Someone please sympathize with how I feel
The childhood that wronged me must be analyze
They hold the real me motionless and I'm paralyzed
Forever in my head being terrorized
Until I come to grips to recognize
I'm the victim who's being destroyed from within
If you give me serious help,
I'll have a chance to win!

WEEPING HEART

Now, the bleedings can't stop
My tear drops fall like rocks
I feel my belly twist in knots
The rage for understanding
In unbreakable locks
My release for steam
Has already popped
Choking for life, I fight to breathe
Emotions of love, I chase to cleave
Outlet for waste
Can't find relief
Suffering without measure
In spite of your belief
Trust, spit in my face
Truth, spray my eyes with mace
Temptation, sit and watch
Decorated in lace
Success, move over to give failure space
Devil, sit and watch,
Victory he tastes
Judgment shows up
Wrong time and place.
Spirit of Angels set me free
Mercy and grace don't forget me
Eyes of blades, Fear can't see
Grave of death, you'll never have me.
Ears hear stories of malign
Who broke the bloodline
The tide that binds
Telling your story with invisible lines
For the real reality
Is only seen by the blind
Sewn mouth of scolds

Cut off the fingers
Of the hands that clothe
Pull out the heart that holds
Then you sucked the life
Out a bare passive soul
Lost in frozen ammonia cold
Molded in time forever to be told
My unconditional love you stole
How can time erase and unfold!

WHO BUT SELF?

Standing strong is the woman in me,
Hidden deep within
Is a child the world can't see.
Fear blackmail's my reality
The part I've known
Is yet to be shown
I'm a victim of an abusive whip
My moment of truth has already slipped
This side of life burnt in dip
Point of no return, once I flipped
The desperation, I'll choose
Mind puzzled with confusions
My world's lost, mangled illusions
How many really heed the warning,
The cry for help that's so annoying?
When you're lost,
There's no one supporting
Feelings of normality aborting
Screaming is the purity
I'm falling fast
Reach, let us be
This one is bad.
The good must flee
My guilt never will be seen,
Unless it satisfies
My own selfish needs.
What I missed I didn't leave,
It was taken,
Rapidly seized!

WHY

Why is it fear you see?
When in your heart you envy me,
God created us all the same,
Slavery is over, I have my name.
Don't you have any remorse?
Where is your shame?
Though clean you think,
When you're covered in stains.
I see your heart,
Dirty as can be.
How can you hate your brother?
Because God set us free.
Stole my people from their homeland,
Forced them to labor
Free maid's hands.
From our roots
Great black leaders,
A strong foundation is paved.
Because of them,
No more will we be slaves.
Today is no different from back then.
You still don't respect
Our black women or men.
The knowledge you fail to learn.
Is our right
This we've earned
I'm tired of being beat,
Awaking in a cold sweat sleep.
Because the pain rips,
Further than endless deep.
Healing has a different stage.
When buried under,
"Over 500 hundred years,"

Soaked in rage…
No matter how much money you paid.
Nothing can make up
What you did to slaves.
We were treated worst than animals in a cage.
Good innocent kids, women and men…
Were burnt in unmarked graves,
Time may move on
But history cannot change.
Every black face you look in
"Is a reflection of that lynched innocence !"

WHY PASS ME BY

Sitting on the side of the road
Holding up my sign
Countless hours I've been here, lost in time.
There you see a cup by me feet,
Thirsting for water and food to eat
Not one dime will you spare
Not a moment of your time,
As if you could care.
Rolling by
While my eyes wail up tears to cry,
Infiltrated by poverty
Robs the very mind of the man you see,
Who can help me break free?
Struggling for that second wind
Wishing for a chance to start again
When you lose everything,
All your respect and then your name
There you sit in an erosion of pain
Even if this whole world was gained.
Misery clouds, all around you rain,
Dripping off the little bit that makes you sane.
The issue should never be your color
God created us all
Reach out and help your brother.
To see someone begging for food
Broken in their spirit,
How can you be so cruel?
Search the inner part of you,
When you help others you don't lose!

WITHERED HAND

Once upon a time I was a young man
With plenty of life,
Not these whitered old hands.
I had all my hair on my head.
I could even make up my own bed.
My voice was strong, my wind was long.
I didn't need a sitter, "I could stay home alone,"
My hearing was sharp as a tack,
Every sound I heard, I could even turn back.
My stomach was tight and flat.
Not like this jelly load of fat.
The family I work hard to take care of.
Now don't even give me any attention, let alone love.
Everyday my opinion is used for a rug.
My true heart is worn like an old pair of shoes.
Mind filled with nothing but the blues.
All the patience I'll ever have.
Now grows old with the past,
My nights are restless, I always feel bad
Visited at night by Mister Sad…
My mood swing comes and goes.
Like I'm a woman on the rag
I look at my fingers that resemble my toes.
Hard, crusty, musty with crinkles and folds.
I've felt of death a time or two, "It's a pinch of cold"
My youth was stolen by father time.
But desires haven't left my mind,
So many young nurses looking so fine.
If I had one good hand,
I would grab their behind.
These withered hands are being erased.
Disperse somewhere out into space.
Another being will take my place,
Thank you, "God for your amazing grace!"

WORDS

What are words
Hard to understand nouns and verbs
If you listen too hard, you haven't heard.
They fall from our lips
A leather wire whip
Invisible marks of shame that slips.
A plunger for our brains
Too familiar slang
Every word births reaction
It doesn't matter your color or name
We have to realize we are all the same
The greatest hurt is no ones gain.
Accidents are correctable
We are only human
We're all capable.
An apology is what you sent
I gladly forgive you is what I meant
Jesus forgives me when I repent.
It's easy to forget
When in judgment we sit.
I'm sorry is a word
That touches people's hearts
A point of healing and a brand new start.
WORDS send a clear message
It never gives hints
And every time it's negative
It leaves tracks and prints

YOU'RE APPRECIATED

When I think back on the old days
Our life seems like a maze
Walls around on every end,
Can't go back to start?
Feels like we're trapped
In a whirl wind…
But You're Appreciated!
How many times
Have you stood behind?
The moments you sacrifice
Your last dime
I know we're still young,
In our prime
Every second counts
Imprinted in our minds.
But You're Appreciated!
When memories force
My dreams to reality
It opens my eyes so I can see
Caged truth cries for relief
Innocence in you wants to run free
Suffocation of forgiveness restrains me
Built on stains that can't be clean
Hidden dangers never to be seen.
You have selfish, righteous,
Black hearted means,
But You're Appreciated!
So many things we lose because
Emotions won't let us love.
We just give up when we fall
Afraid to face life
When it requires your all.
Words unspoken, Treasure unmeasured

On the kindness we abruptly savor
But You're Appreciated!
I see your pain; you shield my tears,
Lost cries buried in passed years.
Personalities so alike,
We must have been cloned
Eye to eye, bone to bone,
To be with each other,
Yet alone…
But You're Appreciated!

YOU WEREN'T THERE

Oh Daddy, where were you
All my searching and I don't have a clue.
The nurturing comfort in your hands.
The day I went to my first dance,
No one to talk to about my boyfriends.
When my mom screams and shouts,
Don't want to hear what I'm talking about.
We get in fights on good days,
All I hear is, you have your dad's ways.
Never ever getting a break
Mother's voice saying so what that's fate.
You're too young, past seven o'clock is late,
It's better if I pick your mate
It may take years but you just have to wait.
Daddy, your voice I hear so clear
The song that dried up all my tears.
Cold sweat nights, you calm my fears.
Nothing should have drove you from me.
A father and daughter were meant to be.
When I look in the mirror it's you I see.
You're the key that unlocks my heart,
Every beat and every part.
You knew "I was your child from the start,"
With you not in my life,
I feel I have been robbed.
Forever wondering in this thick mist of fog.
Daddy, the fact is you left me behind.
I'm buried like stones, lost in time.
I always thought you would be mine.
You can't erase a piece of your soul,
"Tell me, Daddy, what do you hold!"

Printed in the United States
48797LVS00007B/125